Making Peace with Your Past

BY H. Norman Wright:

The Christian Use of Emotional Power
The Living Marriage
Making Peace With Your Past

H. Norman Wright

Making Peace with Your Past

Fleming H. Revell Company
Old Tappan, New Jersey

Library of Congress Cataloging in Publication Data

Wright, H. Norman.
   Making peace with your past.

   Bibliography: p.
   1. Christian life—1960–   . I. Title.
   BV4501.2.W73   1985   248.4   84-17790
   ISBN 0-8007-1228-5

Contents

Acknowledgements

I would like to thank all those who have challenged and stimulated my own thinking and growth through the creation of this work.

I thank my wife, Joyce, for her gracious encouragement and for her acceptance of the clutter, stacks of books, piles of papers, and the preoccupation of my thoughts during the time I was involved in writing this.

I want to express my appreciation and thanks to a friend who has supported, encouraged, and helped me so much during the writing of not only this book but many others. This friend is Marilyn McGinnis, a former student, who in her own right is a highly gifted author. She edits my books, polishing my rough ideas and giving them the flow that is so necessary. Her assistance frees me to create without worrying about the nitty-gritty.

Introduction

The Most Important Journey You May Ever Take

I invite you to come with me on a journey—a journey through life. As we travel we will look at where we have come from, where we are today, and where we will be going. Together we will consider the importance of the past and recognize the role it plays in our present.

I am particularly concerned with helping you look back upon your past because of what it may be able to tell you about yourself. In your passage through life, you want to be fully in charge of the route, the events, and the destination; in order to do so, you need a clear view of where you have been. The amount of control you have depends on whether you live your life as your own person or allow another person within you to direct your energies and thoughts. This "other person" who may be trying to control you is what counselors and psychologists call your "inner child of the past." This inner child is the part of your psyche that retains the burdens and problems of your early days.

As you get better acquainted with your inner child, you will understand yourself in a new and different way. You will have better insight into questions like:

How did I get to be who I am today?
Who is responsible for what I am?
How can I change the parts of me I don't like?

The ideas that follow are the result of twenty years of searching Scripture, counseling hundreds of individuals and couples, and spending hours in research in order to teach graduate students. Other concepts have come from my own thinking, from theologians and pastors and from the prompting and guiding of the Holy Spirit, who has helped me sift through and draw these thoughts together. Indeed, I am convinced that if you know the presence of Jesus Christ in your life, the Holy Spirit is your most powerful resource in making peace with your past. Scripture tells the Christian that he is now an adopted member of God's family. Galatians 4:4, 5 (NAS) tells us that God sent His Son to redeem us from sin, ". . . that we might receive the adoption as sons."

First John 3:1 makes it even more personal: "Behold, what manner of love the Father hath bestowed upon us, that we should be called the sons of God. . . ."

The family into which we have been adopted is quite different from families here on earth, which often have unstable or inconsistent parents. In our Father, God, we have absolute stability and security. We have a parent who is consistently wise and good, and our position as His children is assured.

A. W. Tozer so beautifully described the type of love God has for us when he said, "It is a strange and beautiful eccentricity of the free God that He has allowed His heart to be emotionally identified with men. Self-sufficient as He is, He wants our love and will not be satisfied till He gets it. Free as He is, He has let His heart be bound to us forever."[1]

As you know, when you invited Jesus Christ into your life, the Holy Spirit became a part of your life as well. The Holy Spirit is our teacher and guide, who gives us a greater understanding of how we are related to God. Paul said in Romans 8:15, ". . . But ye have received the Spirit of adoption, whereby we cry Abba, Father." What part does the Holy Spirit play in our adoption? The Spirit makes and keeps us conscious of the fact that we are God's children. The words *Abba, Father,* literally mean that we may call Him "Daddy." The Holy Spirit moves us to look to God as our Father and trust Him as a secure child trusts a dependable parent. This means leaving former childhood patterns that are interfering with the way in which we are currently experiencing life.

With the presence of Jesus Christ in your life today, you can use the ideas that follow to disconnect negative responses that are based in your past. You can become a free person, one who is enjoying life, without heavy anchors from your childhood weighing you down. In spite of events or influences that may have adversely affected you as you grew up, you can still gain control over the inner child who wants to take over. You can still make peace with your past by being reparented by your heavenly Father!

Ask the Holy Spirit to allow the thoughts of these pages to stay in your mind and help you change undesirable beliefs, attitudes, and responses. Begin to practice the things you learn here. Pray for reminders of what you have discovered. Reread again and again the pages that apply to you. Copy significant statements to carry with you. Memorize, meditate on, and visualize the words of God as a guiding force in your life. Thank God that we, as His children, *can* be different.

One more point: as this book takes you on what could be the most important journey you will ever make, you may uncover memories, thoughts, and feelings that have been buried for years. You may sense a strong need to talk to someone especially equipped to help you deal with what you are discovering. Do not hesitate to contact your pastor or a professional Christian counselor in whom you have confidence.

Wherever our journey through life takes us, we can rejoice in the assurance we are not crippled, powerless people. We are new creations who have been adopted into God's family. I do not believe I can overemphasize the importance of the good news that we were "foreordained . . . to be adopted . . . as His own children through Jesus Christ . . ." (Ephesians 1:5 AMP). As you fully grasp this concept and integrate its truths into your life, God will give you the insight, strength, and stability you need not only to live in this world, but to experience life to the fullest, in spite of the stresses and negative influences around you. Too many Christians live as though they were orphans. Thank God each day that you are His and ask Him how He wants you to live—today.

Making Peace with Your Past

1

Excess Baggage—Where Can You Put It?

Some time ago my wife and I had an opportunity to take a cruise on a large ocean liner. Since our itinerary and calendar had been selected for us in advance, our biggest task concerned selecting what we would take with us. As we looked at the pile of goods and clothes strewn on the living-room floor, it was hard to believe that this voyage was to last for only eight days. It looked more like a scene from *Around the World in 80 Days!* We knew that if we were not careful in selecting what we should take with us, we would end up with an incredible amount of excess baggage.

So we began to sort through the pile and ask, *Do we really need this item? Will I ever wear this outfit? What's the purpose of this gadget? Will this item make our journey more enjoyable, or will it get in the way? If I don't have this with me, will I perhaps actually have a better time?* We had to be discriminating. If we took all of that paraphernalia with us on the cruise, we would experience a number of difficulties. For one thing we knew we would have to pay more at the airport for the excess baggage. So my wife and I eliminated much of what we had gathered.

However, even with careful selecting we still took too much. Once we arrived at the ship and the porters brought our luggage to our stateroom, we still had too many suitcases and boxes full of clothes and equipment. We unpacked and hung as much as we could in the closet—but we had brought too many clothes, and they wouldn't fit even if we crammed them in. We went through a selecting process again and put some of our belongings back in the suitcases and boxes.

Then we had a further problem—hiding the luggage. We stashed some of it under the bed, out of the way. That worked fine during the day, but when we wanted to rest or sleep, the bulge in the bed kept us from being as comfortable as we could have been.

Now what to do with the bags that would not fit under the bed? We could leave them in plain sight, which wasn't convenient. We could try to hide them in every nook and cranny of the stateroom. But if you have ever been on a cruise in a postage-stamp size cabin, you know there is *no* spare room!

Ah-ha! What about tossing the items overboard? Then they would be out of sight and gone forever! No more problems and no more irritations! But what a price to pay! We could feel the effects of that action for months and years to come. The baggage would be out of sight, but not out of mind.

There wasn't much we could do about our unwise planning on this cruise, but we both decided that if we ever had it to do again we would make wiser decisions. Because we carried too much baggage we were hindered during our voyage.

Just as my wife and I carried excess baggage on our trip, we may drag along excess luggage on our trip through life. We all start out at birth and sail ahead into childhood, adolescence, and on to adulthood, collecting baggage. And this baggage—the influences and pressures from our parents and other people in our childhood—has a significant bearing upon our adult life. We hang onto much of the excess baggage of our childhood. We are supposed to move out of childhood and become adult. Paul the apostle spoke of this when he said, "When I was a child, I talked like a child, I thought like a child, I reasoned like a child; now that I have become a man, I am done with childish ways and have put them aside" (1 Corinthians 13:11

AMP). However, instead of "putting aside" our "childish ways," we try to carry them with us throughout the voyage, and oftentimes it hinders the process of becoming adult.

How does this childishness reveal itself in adult life? The way a child is treated when he is young—whether that treatment is good or bad—becomes the way he believes he *should* be treated. As he grows, he will perpetuate his elders' actions toward him by incorporating into his actions the responses he learned when he was young. Instead of avoiding the negative inputs from his childhood, he will parent himself in the same unfavorable fashion he is used to experiencing. Unless something intervenes to change his patterns of behavior, he will retain that aspect of his childhood in his adult responses.

Have you ever thought to yourself after saying or doing a particular thing, *That was a childish thing to do?* How did you feel about your action? Did you have a positive feeling, or did you experience chagrin? Did you become critical of yourself for having that thought or feeling? Did you ask yourself, *Where in the world did that come from?* Like the excess baggage on our cruise, these childish things are ghosts from the past. They tend to get in the way when we try to relax and enjoy our life's journey. They are excess baggage.

Excess Baggage

Some of the baggage we accumulated in childhood helps us as adults. Some hinders us and continually creates tension. But whether helpful or hindering, there is security in hanging onto those patterns we learned early on. We remember both the delight and the trauma of being children. We never completely eliminate our childhood experiences or the child within us, as Dr. W. Hugh Missildine describes:

> The child you once were continues to survive inside your adult shell. "Thrive" would perhaps be a better word than "survive," for often this "inner child of the past" is a sprawling, bawling, brawling character, racing pell-mell

into activities he likes, dawdling, cheating, lying to get out of things he doesn't like, upsetting and wrecking others' lives—or perhaps this child is the fearful, timid, shrinking part of your personality.

Whether we like it or not, we are simultaneously the child we once were, who lives in the emotional atmosphere of the past and often interferes in the present, and an adult who tries to forget the past and live wholly in the present. The child you once were can balk or frustrate your adult satisfactions, embarrass and harass you, make you sick—or enrich your life.[1]

Our childish tendencies often emerge when we are exhausted, sick, under a great deal of pressure, have too many responsibilities, or feel threatened. If you are reading this book you are an adult and have both the scars and the credentials to prove it: a birth certificate, driver's license, perhaps a marriage license and even several diplomas. You have had many experiences. As you grow older, wrinkles and gray hairs—and a bit less hair—may give greater credibility to the fact that you are an adult. But just because you manifest all the physical characteristics does not mean that you have "grown up" all the way.

What is a grown-up adult supposed to do and be? You are supposed to be in charge of your own life. This includes making your own decisions, being responsible for your life and carrying out the expectations of adult behavior. Many of us carry this out quite well most of the time. Some of us carry this out some of the time. Others have rare and infrequent flashes of adult behavior, mixed with a lot of childishness. All of us at some time show un-grown-up tendencies. For example, some people are so insecure with making their own decisions that they need the approval and affirmation of others. They are confined in their own personal prison. For some, this need stems from the responses of people currently in their lives. But for a much larger group, the controlling influence is their parents. Their parents may be living or deceased. It really doesn't make that much difference. Even though our parents may be deceased, thousands of miles away, or under the same roof, parental attitudes and admonitions still live within us. We are still at the mercy of their injunctions because, as children, we believed all that they said to us. Consequently, we may find old patterns of response emerging whenever we have contact with them.

What is important is the fact that if you are trying to use other, current relationships to resolve past conflicts with your parents, you may actually be stunting your own growth.

Attachment Baggage

From our earliest days we feel a sense of attachment with our parents. They supply our wants and needs, including a sense of stability. In the same way that we rely on them, we come to rely on childhood patterns, which persist far into adulthood. We may feel very conscious of this and feel immobilized in trying to deal with it, or it could seem a phantom, illusive attachment that still maintains control over our responses. Either way, childhood patterns, whether healthy or painful, are familiar, and familiarity brings security and comfort.

For example, our attraction and attachment to particular people in adulthood can be a carry-over from our past. If our parents were loving, they were bound to leave their stamp upon our lives, even if we cannot remember the specifics of that relationship. Some of us, in adulthood, are drawn to people similar to our parents. Others are drawn to those opposite their parents.

An example of this kind of attachment is Mary. As she dated she seemed to be drawn to men who were not really good for her. She realized that she was drawn to men with some type of flaw. Her own father was a very handsome but passive and ineffective man. From early childhood she greatly admired him and struggled not to see his weaknesses. But after so many years of disappointment, she felt betrayed. Nevertheless, she still chose to date men who were like her father, hoping that they would turn out to be dependable and that she might be able to help them.

John's experience reflects another variation of this tendency. He was raised by a mother who was cold, aloof, and unresponsive. She was extremely neat and was more concerned with her home being a showplace than in nurturing the members of her family. She dressed well and did not want her son to get too close, because he might "mess up her clothes or hair." He felt she used him, because she always told him what to do, how to do it, and what to wear, especially when she entertained. Although John was raised without warmth, love, and nurturing, who does he date again and again? Women who cannot give of themselves and who are little more than unloving mannequins. Why? He keeps trying to refashion women like his mother, in order to make them give him what he needed. He selects women with little potential to give him what he needs and becomes frustrated in his attempts to reform them.

This attachment in dating often continues into mate selection. Some people try to recreate their original family. For example, an only child who has not had much experience relating to his own peer group is more likely to select a parent figure for a spouse. Some people select for a mate a person who is some type of a transference object from their past—someone who is like a parent, sibling, or other significant person with whom they can respond and relate to as they did the person from their past. Most of us do this to some degree. But if there are unresolved emotional issues still existing between us and that significant person from the past, there can be problems. For example, you might choose a partner who is similar to someone you could not get along with in your past. You cannot get along with this type of person in your present situation either. But you are not always aware that you are repeating your old pattern.

All people do not try to recreate their original families when they marry. Many want just the opposite and look for a spouse who is very different. They are trying to escape from their original family and to build some type of new one. They believe they will be more comfortable with this new type of person. But often in their blindness they may overlook buried similarities that emerge later on. When they do discover these in their mates, they may be thrown into a panic, for it appears their history is about to repeat itself. The greater the amount of unresolved issues from their past family situation, the greater the upset.

Why, you may ask, do people turn so much of their lives over to the influence of significant individuals from their past? Would you believe that we really have no choice in the matter? Why not? Because you began your interaction with your parents in a helpless state. You were dependent upon them for your very existence; you learned this very soon. You also learned that there were certain ways you had to respond to maintain a state of well-being with them. If mother and father were happy then you received more positive attention. Over the years children develop quite a repertoire of responses to maintain a good relationship.

As you grew, your physical survival depended less and less upon your parents. But your dependence on your parents for good feelings decreases much more slowly. And for some the decrease is negligible. Dr. Howard Halpern put it so well: "The emotional umbilical cord not only remains uncut but often twists into a Gordian knot that ties us to our parents' reactions to us."[2]

The Powerful Inner Child

Some parents believe that their task is to help their children develop into autonomous, self-sufficient individuals, and they endeavor to bring that about. Others, however, allow their own needs and difficulties to interfere. But both groups are influenced by their own inner child, which gets in their way and prevents them from being fully functioning adults. The videotapes of their own childhood begin to interfere with their proper parental transmissions to their own children. Their own inner child could be threatened by their children's desire to grow and become independent and self-reliant. And what happens? The child's developing inner child interacts with the parent's inner child, and growth is hindered.

Does this mean that I am saying, "Let's lay the blame for all our adult problems and difficulties at the feet of our parents"? Certainly not! Who were your parents? Imperfect humans like you and me. They had their own problems with life and were faced with their own childhood memories. The social and cultural forces of their time affected them, and their own marriage relationship had its effect as well. Because of their own difficulties and filtered perceptions of life, their view of you was perhaps inaccurate, and they did not always respond to you in the best way. We do not always respond to our own children in the best manner, either. You were hurt as a child, in most cases, not because your parents really intended to hurt you, but because they did not know better.

If we give too much importance to the attitudes of our "inner child" that result from the imperfections of our upbringing, then our perception of the present becomes distorted. We find ourselves overreacting, underreacting, or overanalyzing our responses and actions. W. Hugh Missildine says:

> We don't like these feelings and reactions; we don't understand why we have them; we are ashamed of them; we may berate ourselves for having them. Because we have them, we regard ourselves as somehow different, perhaps neurotic. Or, shaken by them, we may try to project the blame for them onto family, friends, fate, even the weather. As they keep recurring, we become increasingly disturbed and may feel ourselves alone, separated from others.[3]

Blaming parents or others for our problems is an excellent way to rid ourselves of responsibility. However, it will not rid us of the problems. But it is a fact that you can break childhood bondage. As adults we can choose to remain the way we are or seek to grow. Our task is not to build a case against our parents, siblings, or others who had an influence on our lives.

Rather, it is to understand who we are and, with the help of Jesus Christ, become free of any damaging results from our past. As we look at the past and open closed doors, we will discover ghosts flitting here and there that disturb and unsettle us. But ghosts cannot hurt us. They are not our enemies. In the next chapter we will begin to lay those ghosts aside as we realize that, as Pogo says, "We have met the enemy, and he is us."

2

How Did You Collect All That Baggage?

When Jim came to my counseling office, he was seeking to stand on his own two feet. His marriage was failing because his wife had gotten tired of making all the decisions for the family. She told Jim that she felt as if she were raising a child rather than enjoying his partnership in their marriage. Jim told me he didn't trust his own decision-making abilities, because, as a child and youth, his parents and older brother and sister had always run interference for him and planned every step of his life.

Jim is a victim of what Dr. W. Hugh Missildine calls "over-coercion." This is just one of several parental attitudes we may have experienced in our childhood, which keep us from becoming grown-up adults. See if you can identify with one or more of the following patterns.[1] If you can, it may help you understand why you experience difficulty in some areas of your adult life, and help you to begin to gain freedom from your past.

Negative Parental Attitudes

Overcoercion is one of the most common parental attitudes. This involves giving a child constant direction, supervision, redirection, instructions, and reminders. In an effort to make things "easy" for their child or to avoid the time and effort it takes to teach a child independence, parents deny him the opportunity to seek and develop his own interests.

In this environment a child has the choice to resist the influence (either overtly or covertly) or to submit and learn to rely upon others for direction. A child who resists overcoercion may manifest his resistance by forgetting, procrastinating, escaping into daydreams, or dawdling. If he learns to submit to overcoercion as a child he can easily follow this pattern of needing outside direction when he becomes an adult, or he may become hard on himself and order and admonish himself as his parents did.

The overcoerced adult has learned to resist his own directives. He becomes a child to his own parental commands. The push-resist cycle of childhood is still functioning.

Oversubmission is the opposite of overcoercion. The oversubmissive parent submits to the child's demands, temper outbursts, and impulsiveness and allows the child to rule and control and become the "boss." He or she may do this out of "love" for the child, but it is not loving, and ultimately harms the child. For the child's response is to become even more demanding, and soon he has no regard for the rights of others. The word *no* is a foreign language to him. He does not learn limits as a child, thus as an adult he still does not comprehend the meaning of the word.

As an adult such a child's goals are often sabotaged by his own impulsive behavior. He can move to excess in eating, smoking, or drinking and is often thoughtless, easily angered, and does not consider the rights of others.

Perfectionism is commonly found in a person who is successful but who is dissatisfied with his level of attainment. Things are never enough or good enough. Where did the perfectionist learn this? usually in a home in which he experienced conditional acceptance. His own parents expected him to perform above and beyond all standards; then acceptance was given. And he cooperated with this dictum by excessive striving and by developing an overserious preoccupation with achievement. He lives with a constant feeling of unworthiness because he does not feel he can meet his parents' standards.

The pattern of belittling oneself follows from childhood right into adulthood. Perfectionists are disappointed in their accomplishments and have little joy in life. Even though other people may be quite satisfied with the perfectionist's accomplishments, their attitude really does not matter.

Overindulgence occurs in an environment where gifts, privileges, and services are lavished upon the child—not because the child needs or wants this attention; his wishes are never taken into consideration. After years of being spoiled, the child becomes bored, loses initiative and spontaneity, and is apathetic. Since he never learned how to work for rewards, his ability to stick with anything and be persistent is nil.

That child now has become an indulged adult. If he is no longer catered to by others, he will either blame life itself or those people who become involved in his life. He will continue to seek people who will cater to his wishes and desires. But when he finds such persons, how does he respond? With boredom, apathy, and so on. The childhood pattern is repeated.

Punitiveness is a parental response that may be manifested in many ways, including out-and-out hostility and aggression toward the child. It is often combined with overcoercion and perfectionism. The parents feel justified in punitive action, but they usually react out of anger, frustration, or impatience rather than any action or attitude of the child. After being the subject of much punitive action, the child may learn to behave in a way that reinforces, justifies, or invites the punishment.

If his parents were negligent as well as punitive, the childish adult may learn to retaliate. Since he has never really experienced enjoyable relationships with others, he may often be overwhelmed with feelings of revenge. On the other hand, if his parents showed affection but were still overly punitive, the childish adult could learn to create situations where he could experience punishment by punishing himself through self-criticism and guilt.

Neglect occurs when parents are either never around or are too preoccupied to become involved with the child at each stage of his or her development. Neglect is found at every level of society. A child who experiences neglect early in life has several possible difficulties to contend with: He may lack the ability to develop close, meaningful relationships with others; he may have difficulty setting limits for himself, because, as a child, no one was ever interested in setting limits for him; he may have difficulty developing a self-identity that assists him in relating to others.

Rejection, believe it or not, is not as common as you would think, at least in the purest sense of the word. It is usually mixed in with another parental response, or the child interprets another response as rejection. A child who is continually rejected develops a poor self-concept. As he grows up he becomes bitter, anxious, and feels isolated, helpless, and of little value.

One way that parents show rejection of a child is to give him too much responsibility. They lay adult responsibilities on him before he is ready for them. As a result, he never has an opportunity to experience being a child, and he longs for what he is missing—acceptance, affection, and praise.

As an adult he may tend to take on too many responsibilities and never learns to relax, play, and enjoy life. Not only does he restrict his own life, but he may tend to place restrictions on the lives of those around him as well.

These are a few of some very common parental attitudes and home environments. Where are you in all this? What influence in your past contributes to who and what you are today?

At the end of this chapter we will ask some questions that will help you determine how much of this excess baggage of your past you are still carrying around with you and how you can begin to dump some of it in a positive, constructive way.

But, first, consider further the environment you grew up in and whether or not you are perpetuating or creating a situation in your home now that is potentially destructive.

Depressogenic Environment

Some children have been brought up in an environment that fosters depression and keeps self-esteem at a low level. This type of home atmosphere, which is contrary to what Christians are called upon to have, is called a "depressogenic environment." Yet many Christians, unfortunately, have created this in their homes by too much emphasis on "thou shalt not," rather than on giving praise and encouragement for the positive things family members do. A depressogenic environment does not provide these important positive needs. It does not provide either a child or an adult with adequate support for his or her self-esteem.

In most cases this environment undermines self-esteem or elicits emotions and conflicts that the person cannot handle. Depression usually results. If we live in an atmosphere of constant attack from someone we love and respect, we are left with feelings of hurt, guilt, and helplessness. And as we become more vulnerable, the verbal and nonverbal exchanges can affect us more and more. Following are some typical attitudes that make up a depressogenic environment.

1. Other people attempt to control us so we cannot gain any type of independence. This control may be subtle or overt, but our lives are directed for us. And in time we begin to believe that we cannot exist without the other person's direction.
2. Others try to convince us that we need them and cannot survive without their emotional support.
3. We are given ambivalent messages that undermine our self-esteem, such as, "In spite of how sloppy you are, we still love you," or, "I guess this is just the burden we will

have to bear, having a problem child like you. But remember, in spite of that, we do care for you."

4. Others attempt to provoke guilt in us by making us feel responsible for situations or conditions. They attempt to make us feel miserable. They can do this without saying a word. A parent can come into the room, look around to see how clean it is, look disgusted, sneer, shake his or her head, and leave. What kind of feelings could that arouse in a person?

5. Our intentions and motives can be misinterpreted by significant others. We can begin to doubt our own perceptions. Constant questions such as the following can accomplish this: "Are you sure you said that or did that?" or, "I'm not sure anyone else heard you say that . . . ," or, "You don't really mean that, of course." Hearing these statements enough can create doubts.

6. If the communication process was blocked in our homes, both rejection and indifference occurred. A relationship where deep and significant feelings cannot be expressed will hinder growth.

7. Competitiveness in a family relationship can cause depression and/or lowered self-esteem. Anything that is done to build envy or jealousy can have a detrimental effect upon the family. If we were compared with other children or another child was given more attention, we were affected.

8. If the home is void of joy and humor and maintains a constant monotony, we may wonder about ourselves: *Am I the cause of this dull life? Why are my efforts to add variety and new activities not accepted?* If we receive few or no positive responses, we learn that it isn't safe to share.

9. If we were not allowed to display any anger as we were growing up, we probably learned to block this and other emotional expression as well. We may also have channeled our anger into depression.[2]

What Do We *Do* With the Excess Baggage?

Depression attitudes like those just described can leave us with an inner child who is carrying a great deal of excess baggage that we constantly have to walk around or trip over at the most unlikely times. If we are aware of those childhood tendencies and attempt to hide them under the bed, we still experience their presence when we need to rest and relax. So the powerful inner child causes aches and pains during our waking hours as well as during the hours of rest.

Some of us acknowledge this excess baggage but attempt to hide it in the closet. But one day we have to open the closet. There we are—face-to-face one more time. We may try to rearrange the issues, but this doesn't resolve their continuing influence upon our daily lives.

Can you throw the excess baggage of the inner child overboard and eliminate its influence? Can you really eliminate all of the influence and experiences of your childhood? Is it possible to rid yourself and start anew? Of course not. We cannot vanquish the powerful inner child, but we can identify him and begin to correct our negative attitudes about him. We need to treat ourselves with the same regard God has toward us. We can give up any resentments and bitterness we hold toward significant people from our past and realize that we can become grown-up adults. Our memories will always be with us, but their effect can be diminished. Christians have this capability. We can become positive parents to ourselves.

Reconstruct Your Past

Use your memories as the key to understanding your past and the influence your inner child has had on your emotions and reactions as an adult. To gain a greater awareness and understanding of your childhood development, first ask yourself questions such as: *What was I really like as a child? What were my parents' reactions toward me? What were my reactions to my parents' responses to me?*

To help you recall some of these memories get a pencil and paper and find a comfortable chair to sit in. Begin to reconstruct your childhood from the earliest age that you can remember. Some have found it helpful to look through childhood picture albums, which can activate forgotten memories. Keep paper and pen with you at all times. Other memories will emerge during the day, when you least expect them. The more you recall, the more helpful it can become. We can all remember isolated times when we were lonely, afraid, angry, rejected, and so on. What you are looking for, however, are prevailing, continual patterns. Try to discover the consistent day-to-day attitudes you perceived others had toward you.

As you go through this reconstructed journey in your attempt to touch your memories, be aware of the feelings that each memory raises. Because of some intense pain from these experiences, some memories may have barriers and blockades surrounding them. But if the pain remains, these memories are still alive and affecting you. Allow the feelings to surface. Avoid getting stuck on one memory, however. You may, because of the pain, find yourself returning to dwell upon it time and time again, once it has surfaced. You may overanalyze it and try to understand what happened. You may spend an inordinate amount of time attempting to prove to yourself that you were not to blame for whatever happened.

If the pain is coming from one or just a few isolated incidents, it may keep you from clearly seeing the overall broad picture of your childhood. You are looking for themes or patterns that were fairly constant in your life, and you also want to know what your consistent response was to your environment.

Your goal is to discover how your past and present relate. Your reactions to people in work situations, to your marriage partner, or to your friends may be founded in attitudes and methods of response you learned in childhood. Either use your present patterns to determine your past influences or work forward from your childhood to gain greater understanding about these habits.

The following questions and directions will help you in your reconstruction:

1. What were your moods as a child?
2. Were you happy, and if so, when?
3. Think of times when you were demanding, when you felt sorry for yourself or felt lonely.
4. Recall times when you purposely tried to elicit approval from your parents and how you tried to do this. What were the times when they gave you their approval, and how did you feel?
5. What were your fears, and who knew about those fears?
6. How did others respond when you told them you were afraid?
7. How did your brother or sister respond to you on a consistent basis?
8. What was your father's day-by-day and week-by-week attitude toward you?
9. What was your mother's continuous response and reaction?
10. Were they strict, indulgent, moralistic, demanding?
11. Did they demand perfection from you?
12. Were you catered to in any way?
13. It is also important to remember how you reacted to these responses of others. Did you "buy" everything that was said to you?
14. Did you attempt to conform to every request?
15. Did you comply with others' expectations and requests?
16. What was your attitude like?
17. Were you disrespectful?
18. Did you become angry or sullen?
19. How did other people respond to your anger or sullenness?
20. Did you learn to use or work your parents to get your way?
21. What was your home atmosphere like? Happy, loving, tense, bickering, silent, depressogenic?

22. As you continue your search for memories of your past, ask yourself these questions about both of your parents. Did he/she have time for me?
23. Was he/she home much of the time?
24. Could I approach him/her with my problems or difficulties?
25. How did he/she react?
26. And how did I handle the reaction?
27. What were/are the positive qualities of each parent?
28. What were/are the negative qualities of each parent?
29. Describe how you felt/feel about each parent.
30. What emotions did/does each parent express?
31. Describe how each parent communicated/communicates with you.
32. Describe your most pleasant and unpleasant experience with each parent.
33. What messages did each parent give to you in your early childhood and during your adolescence?
34. What are the messages today?
35. How did you react to those messages?
36. Describe how each parent punished you.
37. How did each parent share criticisms with you?
38. How did you feel when this occurred?
39. In what ways are you similar to your father?
40. In what ways are you different from your father?
41. In what ways are you similar to your mother?
42. In what ways are you different from your mother?
43. Was your relationship with your mother close or distant during childhood?
44. What has it been like during the past ten years?
45. Was your relationship with your father close or distant during childhood?
46. What has it been like during the past ten years?
47. Did you have brothers or sisters?
48. If so, what was your relationship with them then, and what is it like now?

These relationships are important, but not as much as those with your parents. But if your siblings' attitudes affected your parents' attitudes toward you, they may be very important. If you were the scapegoat or culprit whenever there were squabbles, then you developed certain attitudes.

49. Consider your life today and then relate it to your past. In what situations do you feel the most uncomfortable?
50. Do these have any similarities to your past experiences?
51. In what situations is your anger excessive or inappropriate?
52. Are these times reminders of situations in your past?
53. Is this the way in which you responded as a child?
54. When do you experience fear or anxiety?
55. Who is present when fear or anxiety occurs?
56. How do these times remind you of experiences of your past?
57. Do you ever feel embarrassed and, if so, under what conditions?
58. When were you embarrassed as a child?
59. Who embarrassed you the most?
60. In what situations do you feel most self-conscious? Why?
61. When did this same situation occur in the past?
62. When do you feel alone?
63. Is this a new feeling or one from the past that continues to haunt you?
64. Who are the people today you have the greatest difficulty in relating to?
65. Are they in any way similar or dissimilar to significant people in your past?
66. Are you reacting in your adult life as an adult, or has your child response continued to emerge and live your life for you?
67. Are you borrowing responses from your past, or have you developed your own healthy responses so that you are a free person?

Two final questions for your reconstruction: In what way is the presence of Jesus Christ in your life disconnecting your responses from your past to the present? Are you becoming a free person and one who is living your present life without heavy anchors from the past slowing you down?

Perhaps you have not yet applied Jesus Christ to your life in this area of your past. You can ask Him to free the blockage from your mind, so you have greater understanding and awareness of your past experiences. You can ask Him for clarity of thought in accurately recalling those memories. Ask Him to help you identify how you continue to treat yourself as others treated you in early years.

Jesus Christ came to set us free—free from the consequences of sin and death, but also free from the crippling patterns and experiences of the past.

Now that you have reconstructed your past, in the next chapter you will learn how you can change the way you have been responding and move toward being a grown-up adult.

3

"Me, Change? Impossible"—Or Is It?

As I guide people in peeling away the layers of the past a standard question almost always surfaces: "Do you think I can really change? What good will all this remembering of my childhood and my parents' mistakes really do?"

Often, what the questions really mean is: "I'm not sure I want to change. I have my problems, but I'm handling them. Digging around in my feelings and memories could make things worse, not better."

I sympathize with these statements. They reveal a certain amount of discomfort and even fear. But I know, from counseling with many of those in such situations, that dealing with the inner child of the past is well worth the effort.

Paul, a forty-year-old executive, told me: "For years I limped through life. Other people saw me as happy, successful, and satisfied. What a joke! My life was pain—just pain inside. And I was very clever at hiding it from my friends. I moved through life smiling on the outside and agonizing on the inside. I felt hopeless that my inner life would ever change. For years it did not change. But now I can tell you that a person does not have to go through life with crippling hurts and memories of the past controlling his life. It did begin to change, gradually at first, but now I am free to live as God wants me to live."

Paul found a way to free himself from the crippling hurts of the past. You may be feeling as Paul did at first, that you too are stuck and that hope is a fleeting mist. But keep reading. There is hope indeed.

Change is possible for believers in Christ because our faith is an inward transformation, not just an outward conformity. Yet for many people outward conformity seems to be all they can achieve. The plan that God has for our lives creates an inward change, which then moves outward. When Paul says, "My little children, of whom I travail in birth again until *Christ be formed in you* ..." (Galatians 4:19, *italics added*), he is telling us that we have to let Jesus Christ live life *in* and *through* us.

In Ephesians 4:23, 24 we are told, "And be renewed in the spirit of your mind; ... put on the new man, which after God is created in righteousness and true holiness." The new man has to be put on from the inside. We are able to put on the new man because God has placed Jesus Christ within us. We are to let Him work within us. This means we must give Him access to our memory banks and the past experiences that need to be relinquished.

I Want to Change, But . . .

"Yes," you say, "I want to make changes in my life. But I'm afraid." Let's see for a moment why people are afraid of change.

First of all, there is stability in living your life just the way it is, and you disrupt this stability when you make a change. Change, however, is a part of life. It is inevitable. Isn't it better to plan for the change and have a voice in what takes place? Why pretend that you can prevent it? You should be able to see change not as an enemy but as an opportunity for growth and maturity.

Some people are afraid to change because they do not want to appear fickle. They are overly concerned about what others will think and say about them.

Still other people believe that changing is admitting failure. They will have to admit to themselves and perhaps to other people, "The way I have been living life is wrong," and they hate admitting that they are wrong. Yet it is actually a sign of maturity to admit that you want your life to be different. Changing means that you are preparing for the future, that you are adapting to new situations, and that you desire growth. Your world is changing, and you want to keep up with it and even affect some of its change.

Some people resist change because they don't want to be controlled or scheduled. Change should be spontaneous, they feel. It should "just flow" from us and not be something we have to plan. But whether or not we are aware of it, we make large and small choices all day long. We are not as spontaneous and free as we would like to think.

Some people are fearful of experimenting. Change is risky, and there are no guarantees as to the outcome. Some changes can make matters worse, but that is part of the risk. Actually, the likelihood that *positive* changes can take place—if you follow the suggestions in this book—is quite high. If change is to occur, you need to be flexible and willing to run a risk. It is far riskier staying stuck in the same pattern all your life. If you are totally satisfied with your life now, you may not want to change. But are you sure there isn't a better way to live? Why not at least try something new? And if you are a believer in Christ, you already have a head start toward change.

When you accepted Christ, you became a new creation in Jesus Christ. You are now identified with Him. Paul in 2 Corinthians 5:17 says: "Therefore if any man be in Christ, he is a new creature: old things are passed away; behold, all things are become new." Then in Romans 6:6 (NAS): ". . . Our old self was crucified with Him . . . that we should no longer be slaves. . . ."

By believing in Jesus Christ, we have died with Him and have been raised a new creation with Him. All things are new. In what way are you new today? How can your mind—your thought life—the influence of past experiences become new in your life now? First Corinthians 2:16 tells us, ". . . We have the mind of Christ." In 1 Corinthians 1:30 we read, "But of him are ye in Christ Jesus, who of God is made unto us wisdom, and righteousness, and sanctification, and redemption." You and I have the *wisdom* of God. Put this thought together with the fact that we have the mind of Christ: *Not only do I have the mind of Christ, but I also have God's wisdom to apply in using the mind of Christ in my life.*

This is very important. Why? Because one of the struggles in which we all engage is with the ghosts of our past. Scripture speaks of this as the "old self" (Romans 6:6 NAS). The mind of our old self has been programmed with our early experiences. But even before this we came into life with a mind that has been affected by the fall of man. Thus we begin life with a mind that has a propensity toward negative thinking, worry, fear, guilt, and remembering experiences that would be better off relinquished. Even when we become believers, the residue—the ghost—of old thinking is still with us. It tends to bring its influence into play with our wills, our emotions, our thoughts, and our behavior.

Our hurts from the past are like abscesses—raw, hemorrhaging wounds that become covered by scabs. But from time to time the scabs peel off. Unfortunately, what is uncovered is not the complete growth of restored life, but the same bleeding sore.

Many people travel through life with such unhealed emotional wounds. They carry them in their memories. The capacity for being affected by our past actually increases with age, for the older we get, the more we have to remember. Our life in one degree or another is a reflection of our memories. The feelings we have at the present time—such as joy, sorrow, anger, grief, and contentment—are more dependent upon the way we remember an event than the event itself. The greater the length of time between the event and the present, the greater the potential for distortion. Who we are today is a product of how we remember past events. Recently I heard Dr. Lloyd Ogilvie describe this condition, in a Sunday-morning message. He said:

> We mortgage the future based upon what happened in the past. We have positive memories of the past which we can't imagine could ever be repeated and we have negative memories which we know will be repeated.
>
> Often we become the image of what we remember instead of what we envision for the future.

Healing Painful Memories

Our emotions and their intensity are related to memory. Henri Nouwen said, "Remorse is a biting memory, guilt is an accusing memory, gratitude is a joyful memory and all such emotions are deeply influenced by the way we have integrated past events into our way of being in the world. In fact, we perceive our world with our memories."[1]

Did you ever think of the possibility that much of the suffering of a person's life comes from memories? How do these memories emerge? as feelings—feelings of loneliness, insecurity, fear, anxiety, suspiciousness. The reason they hurt is because they tend to be mostly buried and emerge only when they choose. The more painful these memories are, the more hidden and repressed they become. They hide, as it were, in a corner of the deepest cavern of our minds. Because they are hidden, they escape healing.

What do you do with a painful memory? You may try to forget it, or you may act as though it did not occur. Trying to forget the pains of the past gives these memories power and control over your life, and you proceed through life dragging a weight. You become a walking emotional cripple. You attempt to edit your own personal history and try to selectively remember, but there is a twofold cost: You continue to limp through life, and you miss out on an opportunity to grow and mature.

This need not be. A painful memory can become a healed gift instead of a searing reminder. How does healing occur? By facing your memories, remembering them, letting them out of their closet. Henri Nouwen said, "What is forgotten is unavailable and what is unavailable cannot be healed."[2]

The healing of an intensely painful memory is difficult because of the defenses we have built around it to keep us from directly confronting that ghost from the past. In our minds we raise a drawbridge to keep the enemy out, but we end up keeping others away from us as well. This limits us from enjoying deep intimacy, trust, and love. Raising the drawbridge does not make our castle more secure, rather it turns our sanctuary into a dungeon. To heal our hurts of the past, we must lower the drawbridge by giving up our defense mechanisms and confronting the painful memories.

We can let down the drawbridge because of the presence of Christ in our lives. He gives us two possibilities for growth and happiness: First, He changes the old patterns by eliminating the effects of harmful memories. Second, He helps us use our minds, emotions, and wills to behave in a new, more positive way both now and in the future.

Our task then, through Christ, is to remove the rough edges and fissures that drain our energy and keep us from moving forward. Christ is the Master Sculptor who renews us after His image (*see* Colossians 3:10).

> When a fanatic dealt several damaging blows to Michelangelo's Pieta, the world was horrified. It surprised no one when the world's best artists assembled to refashion the disfigured masterpiece.
>
> When sculptors arrived in Italy, they didn't begin repairing the marred face immediately. Rather they spent months looking at the Pieta, touching the flowing lines, appreciating the way each part expressed suffering yet ecstasy. Some spent months studying a single part such as the hand until finally the sculptors began to see more and more with the eyes of Michelangelo and to touch and feel as the master artist would have done. When the sculptors finally began repairing the face, the strokes belonged almost as much to Michelangelo as to themselves.

Not Michelangelo's but rather God's sculpturing hand fashioned us from soil-dust into a masterpiece which surpassed even the Pieta (Gen. 2:7). It should not surprise us that God constantly refashions us—that as soon as we disfigure ourselves, He's already sculpturing the pieces back together.

When we ask for healing, we shouldn't immediately rush into it. Rather, we should start knowing ourselves as does our Sculptor. We don't see the depth of our need for healing until we know our infinite value. The least self-centered blow destroys more than any blow to the Pieta. "We are God's work of art created in Christ to live the good life as from the beginning He meant us to live it" (Eph. 2:8). When we thank God for the gifts He gives us, we begin to see ourselves no longer from our own eyes but from His. If we know our giftedness, then we know how we require healing and thus we can become all that our Sculptor envisions.[3]

In order to let the Master Sculptor work on us, we need to see what went into the making of who we are now. Our view of ourselves began in infancy. Smiles or frowns, slaps or pats, reaffirming or sarcastic comments from our parents and others were all filed in our emotional memory banks. These memory banks become our warehouses of beliefs, feelings, and impressions upon which we draw throughout our lifetime. Some items in our memory banks are potentially harmful, and they will stay with us unless we take definite steps to replace them with others. Some people's memory banks send them into the world with many pluses, and life is good to them. Others' memory banks send them out with deficits, and life is a constant struggle.

The image that is formed by words and actions of others throughout our childhood reflects how we see ourselves—as worthy or unworthy of respect and love, competent or useless, likable or distasteful, successful or a failure. We tend to respond according to what is stored in our memory banks. One father noticed that when visitors came to their home he became short and impatient with his children. As he talked about this with me he discovered that his problem was not so much impatience with his children as it was fear of rejection by the visitors if his children did not behave and measure up to standards he set for them. Where did this fear come from? From his own past experiences of rejection.

Janet shared with me that she usually contradicted her husband, Bill, when he complimented her. She could not seem to accept his positive statements. This was very frustrating to Bill. As she was contradicting him one day, she began to remember comments her parents had made to her. They told her not to believe positive statements that others said about her, because those people just wanted to use her in some way. They also told her the statements were not true anyway, because she didn't have anything to offer. These painful memories blocked her ability to accept her husband's love and care.

Whenever John talked to his wife, he would get loud and angry if she happened to turn her head or look away for any reason. He could not understand why he became irate at her seeming inattention. During a prayer session one day, he remembered that his mother rarely listened to him and usually left the room when he was talking. His fear of not being listened to by his wife came from his experience with his mother. Through prayer and talking this through with his wife, he was able to put those experiences and memories in perspective.

We may already be aware of a particular memory and its effect on us. But sometimes it may take some digging to search it out. Psychologists and counselors are often instrumental in helping people uncover painful memories. But, as a Christian, you can call on another source. You can call upon the Holy Spirit to bring to mind the disturbing memories that need to be healed. You do this through a quiet time of praying, asking the Holy Spirit to reveal the situation that created the memory in the first place. He may show you the first incident that occurred, or He may show you the first time you responded to the original event.

As you make your request in prayer you then need to sit quietly, allowing free-floating thoughts to come to your awareness. You should not *try* to make thoughts emerge, but rather relax and allow the Holy Spirit to work. If you are attempting to discover situations from the past that correspond to present responses, you could take one person at a time from your childhood and ask "Did this ever occur with my mother [father, sister, brother, and so on]?"

The Holy Spirit may reveal a pattern in your behavior with many people. And as you trace this pattern back you can discover the origins. You are not looking for the source in order to blame yourself or anyone else. Remember the story of Michelangelo's *Pieta?* You are looking at your own memories to allow the artistry of the Holy Spirit to correct the blemishes.

When a memory is discovered, your first request to the Lord is to give you the grace to thank Him for that memory. As painful as it may be, you need this discovery. Indeed, it is an emancipation! You are experiencing the first step toward freedom. You now have the unique opportunity to be free from the control of the past.

But the experience can also be a bit frightening. Fortunately, we do not go through it alone, for God is with us. We can consider the hurt of the past as tragic and permanently crippling emotionally. In other words, we can choose to be a slave to it or to be freed from it. Paul says, "So then, brethren, we are under obligation, not to the flesh, to live according to the flesh—" (Romans 8:12 NAS), and, "It was for freedom that Christ set us free; therefore keep standing firm and do not be subject again to a yoke of slavery" (Galatians 5:1 NAS).

There is freedom in the Spirit, and it comes from Jesus Christ, who went to the cross for our sins, our emotions, and our memories as well. "What then? Shall we sin because we are not under law but under grace? May it never be!" (Romans 6:15 NAS). Being alive to Christ, fully alive, means being dead to our memories of pain.

Take It Slow and Easy

The healing of memory may be immediate, but often it is progressive. Inner healings can take months or even years. The greater the amount of buried material, the slower the process. This is healthy. We are limited in what we can confront at one time. It could be that experiencing all the hurt of the experience at once would be intolerable. We can only handle one draining sore at a time, and when that is healing, we can move to the next.

Another reason for facing one memory at a time is that you need to develop new ways of responding and behaving. John, the man who got angry because his wife turned away from him when he talked to her, needs to understand that she really is interested in what he has to say. Then he can respond accordingly. Janet, who contradicted her husband's compliments, needs to accept his statements as genuine expressions of his love for her.

Like a child, your first steps may be halting and tentative. Attempting too much at once could discourage you. As you establish new thoughts and ways of behaving you are encouraged to confront additional areas. When you become fully aware of a painful memory, the intensity of the hurt will diminish a little each day as you think about it. Soon it is no more than an historical remembrance. The more you are willing to express thankfulness and forgiveness, the sooner the hurt will leave.

Praise Is a Healer

I would like to suggest another element involved in change, with which you may not be familiar. It's called praise. Praise for what God has done, for who He is, and for what He will do, releases to Him the tight control we have had on our own lives.

It is easy to praise God for what He *has done,* because we can reflect back and measure the actual results. We have something tangible, and there is little risk involved.

But what about the future? How difficult is it for you to praise God for what He is *going to do?* Such praise opens your life to some possibilities you may have never considered. By praising God, you not only become a risk taker, but you become more aware of what He wants for you. This may be an uncomfortable idea for you. It may mean that you praise God in an unpleasant job situation or during a difficult financial position. It may mean praising God in spite of that taxing personal relationship you have in your marriage or family life. Perhaps you are troubled and perplexed about some situation. That is exactly when God wants you to praise Him.

Where there appear to be no answers, no solutions, and you face an immovable mountain, why not praise Him? What have you got to lose? You have already run out of your own answers. Why not admit it and look elsewhere for solutions with an attitude of acceptance? As I wrote these words to you the thought struck me, *Why don't you do that yourself, right this moment?* I am presently facing a crisis with my ministry organization and with making some difficult decisions. And so right now I just practiced what I am suggesting to you. I praised God for being with me in the situation, the difficulty, the roadblocks, and for this crossroads. Now, even though I am a bit fearful of making the wrong decisions, I am waiting upon Him and am experiencing a sense of peace.

Lloyd Ogilvie has an interesting thought along this line: "Consistent praise over a period of time conditions us to receive what the Lord has been waiting patiently to reveal to us or release for us."[4]

We readily thank people after the fact or if we have a guarantee that they will help us out of the predicament according to our plan. But to put our future in the hands of someone we cannot see or touch and say, "Whatever You bring about in this matter, I praise You," is not typical. We are guarantee-oriented people, not risk takers. We resist, rebel, and grate at the thought of praising God in every situation.

But think about it for a while before you discount the advice to give thanks "in every thing" (1 Thessalonians 5:18). We have read and heard this passage presented dozens of times and perhaps ignored it. But it just sits there and doesn't go away. On occasion, we grasp at it during times of panic. But what if this principle of praise became as regular as our daily eating? What might happen to us? It is worth a try.

But first of all, consider who it is that you are praising. Who is God to you? To some, God is a figment of man's imagination. To others a stone deity. Who is your God? What is your concept of God? A proper concept of God is basic to your existence and to practical daily Christian living.

The best definition of God that has lasted over the years is still found in the Westminster Shorter Catechism. In answer to the question, "What is God?" the reply is, "God is a Spirit, infinite, eternal, and unchangeable in his being, wisdom, power, holiness, justice, goodness and truth." Why were you created? To know God. What can bring you more contentment, joy, delight, and peace than anything else? It is the knowledge of God.

> Thus says the Lord, "Let not a wise man boast of his wisdom, and let not the mighty man boast of his might, let not a rich man boast of his riches; but let him who boasts boast of this, that he understands and knows Me, that I am the Lord who exercises lovingkindness, justice, and righteousness on earth; for I delight in these things," declares the Lord.
>
> Jeremiah 9:23, 24 NAS

Do you understand what is involved in knowing God? James Packer says it is:

> ... listening to God's word and receiving it as the Holy Spirit interprets it, in application to oneself; second, noting God's nature and character, as His word and works reveal it; third, accepting His invitations, doing what He commands; fourth, recognizing, and rejoicing in, the love that He has shown in thus approaching one and drawing one into this divine fellowship.[5]

We are to recognize and rejoice in Him. We are therefore, first of all to praise who God is as a response to His love, His goodness, His faithfulness, and His unbelievable concern for each one of us. If we praise God, we are recognizing His sovereignty and His capability. In praising God we are making a transfer—giving trust and dependence to Him, rather than trusting and depending upon our own efforts and abilities.

Imagine someone sending you a letter admonishing you twenty times to rejoice—and four of those times to rejoice always? Well, that is the type of letter Paul wrote to the church at Thessalonica. When you and I rejoice in the Lord, we do not do it because we feel like it, it is an act of our will, a commitment. When we rejoice in the Lord, we begin to see life from another point of view. Praise is our means of gaining a new perspective and new guidance for our bogged-down lives. You may be thinking that you are too busy during the day to stop and praise God. That is just the time to do it, when you are too busy, fretful, and overwhelmed. Stop, clear your mind, and praise God. You will feel refreshed.

Praising God in advance of a solution is an act of faith, a way of saying, "I don't know the outcome, but I am willing to trust."

> Praising the Lord makes us willing and releases our imaginations to be used by Him to form the picture of what He is seeking to accomplish. A resistant will makes us very uncreative and lacking in adventuresome vision in the use of our capacity of imagination. God wants to use our imagination in the painting of the picture of what He is leading us to dare to hope for and expect. We become what we envision under *the Spirit's guidance.* That's why our own image of ourselves, other people, our goals, and our projects all need the inspiration of our imagination. However, until the Holy Spirit begins His work releasing it, our will keeps our imagination stunted and immature.[6]

Praise makes a difference because it is an act of relinquishment. This allows God to help us get ready for the next step. I am not just talking about crisis praying, but the development of a consistent pattern of praise. Praising means that we thank Him for the fact that the answer is coming, and we will wait for it. We need God's perspective of our lives and the solutions we are seeking. This perspective can come through praise.

Praise is a healer of painful memories. Change is possible, especially for those of us who are new creations in Christ.

Next we will discuss another aid to making peace with the past—imaging.

4

Imaging to Heal the Past

Daydreams have been responsible for some of our greatest discoveries. Thomas Edison did not just sit down and invent the light bulb. He first lay on the couch in his workshop and filled his mind with fantasies. Debussy created some of his music by viewing reflections of the sun on a river. Fantasy can rescue us from daily doldrums or lead us to invent a machine; one is tied to escape, the other to accomplishment. Fantasy can also be used to help heal your detrimental memories and free you from self-condemnation.

For example, I have talked to many Christians who have confessed their sins to God, asked Him to forgive them, and in some cases even made restitution. They realize intellectually that God has forgiven them, but emotionally they do not feel forgiven. They still feel unworthy and guilty. I usually suggest that they do the following imagery exercise to help them find the freedom from guilt they seek.

"Sit back in your chair and close your eyes. Visualize a large blackboard with a mass of meaningless words and phrases written on it. As you look more closely this mass of words begins to spell out the acts or behaviors for which you do not feel forgiven. They now stand out clearly and boldly among the other words and phrases.

"Now visualize Jesus Christ standing at the board. He is sweeping a damp sponge across that blackboard, wiping it clean. He keeps on until it is so clean that something fresh and new and meaningful can be written on it. God is erasing your past sin and failures so you can start again.

"Now visualize Jesus beckoning you to come to the blackboard. He asks you to place your hand in His, and He says, 'I want you to see that the board has really been wiped clean. Feel My hand cleaning the board and believe that it is becoming clean and new again.' You feel His hand cleaning the board, and now it begins to dawn on you: Jesus is actually doing this for you.

"Then visualize Jesus turning to you, placing His hand on your shoulder, and saying, 'You are forgiven. Experience my forgiveness as a part of your life. Live your life as a forgiven person.' By this action He is also telling you to forgive yourself, for there is no need to keep count of the errors on the blackboard. They no longer exist. It is as though someone hit the erase button on the calculator."

You may need to run this picture and sequence through your mind again and again until, through imaging, you experience the acceptance and forgiveness that are yours.

The Power of Imagination

Fantasy is a characteristic only of human life. It is our ability to imagine that sets us apart from animals. Cats, dogs, and birds do not imagine a situation being different from what it is.

Our fantasies or images can be a form of escape leading us away from responsibilities, pain, or disillusionment. Or they can be powerful magnets drawing out our abilities and strengths to unlock problems and tear down barriers blocking our progress.

Imagination is the creative function within us, and it is a

necessary part of life. We vary in how much we use our imaginations and the way in which we use them, but we all use them to some degree.

Our minds can create images so realistic they chart the direction we choose to move, for our actions and feelings begin there. Imagery can be used to bring about the positive changes we seek in our lives.

The finest description of imaging I have read is the following:

> Imaging, the forming of mental pictures or images, is based on the principle that there is a deep tendency in human nature to ultimately become precisely like that which we imagine or image ourselves as being. An image formed and held tenaciously in the conscious mind will pass presently, by a process of mental osmosis, into the unconscious mind. And when it is accepted firmly in the unconscious, the individual will strongly tend to have it, for then it has you. So powerful is the imaging effect on thought and performance that a long-held visualization of an objective or goal can become determinative.[1]

There are many people today whose first response to the challenges of life is one of these: "I can't do that." "It's over my head." "If I try that, I will fail." Their feeling of inferiority limits their efforts and keeps them caged and shackled. Yet God is present in the life of every believer who feels inferior, as well as those who do not. How can you release the power of God within you? What can help you begin to take risks?

Imaging and prayer, followed with action, are the keys. Picture yourself facing some overwhelming situation, with Jesus standing beside you. He takes the first step forward. See yourself taking one step to bring yourself up beside Jesus. He takes another step, and you again move up beside Him. Saturating your mind—imaging the presence of God, can free you from the fear of failure. It takes time, work, and effort, as the Scripture tells us: "... Gird up ... your minds" (1 Peter 1:13). *Gird* literally means "mental exertion."

Imaging is a positive thinking carried one step further. In imaging, one does not merely think about a hoped-for goal; one "sees" or visualizes it with tremendous intensity, reinforced by prayer. Imaging is a kind of laser beam of the imagination, a shaft of mental energy in which the desired goal or outcome is pictured so vividly by the conscious mind that the unconscious mind accepts it and is activated by it. This releases powerful internal forces that can bring about astonishing changes in the life of the person who is doing the imaging.[2]

Healing Through Imagination

Our thoughts and beliefs have a direct influence upon our bodies. If we deliberately change our thoughts, we may be able to deliberately change our bodies as well. Examples of this can be seen in the research concerning the relationship between repressed anger and ulcerative colitis, difficulty in crying and asthma, and superachievers and asthma. Our belief system can have a direct bearing upon our health.

Imagery is used within the medical profession for the healing of disease. There are some people who are able to use this power to bring about dramatic effects and changes in their bodies. Some oncologists have used imagery with their cancer patients. It has also been used with other physical disorders as a motivational tool for recovering health. The treatment follows a series of definite steps.

The patient is given the following instructions:

1. Find a quiet spot where you can sit without fear of interruption. Sit comfortably, with your feet on the floor.
2. Focus on the rhythm of your breathing. Concentrate on this.
3. Relax and recognize that you are in a quiet place. Visualize the tensions as knots or tourniquets. See them coming undone.

4. Systematically tense your muscles and release them as you are guided over your body.
5. Picture yourself in an ideal spot for relaxation. See all the scenery, hear the sounds, smell all the aromas. (This process continues for several minutes.)
6. Create a mental image of the ailment or the pain which is bothering you.
7. Visualize the treatments you are receiving and see them attacking the ailment or helping the body to heal itself.
8. Picture the body's healing powers at work overcoming the ailment.
9. See yourself strong, healthy and free from pain.
10. Visualize yourself moving towards your goals in life.
11. See yourself going through this experience three times a day and the accessions of strength that come to you.
12. Gradually open your eyes and go back to your normal activities.[3]

An arthritic patient is asked to visualize his joints, seeing the irritation and granules on their surfaces. He then visualizes the white blood cells coming in, picking up the granules and then smoothing over the rough surfaces. An ulcer patient visualizes his stomach with the pockets in the lining and the soreness. In his mind he visualizes the soothing effect of the medicine and his diet. He then images the healthy cells as they multiply and the white cells doing their cleansing work. He visualizes life becoming free from pain.

High blood pressure patients also make use of this technique. They practice relaxation exercises as well as imagery. In their imagery they see their blood vessels as pipes. They visualize their muscles tightening and making the pipes narrower, so the blood has more difficulty getting through. Then they see their medication relaxing the muscles so the heart has an easier time in its work of pumping the blood through these vessels.

Imagery is used more and more today for the purpose of

pain control. Guided imagery has proven to be a safe and effective way of raising an individual's tolerance to pain as well as freeing up the nervous system to maximize the healing processes of the body.

(For additional information contact the Bresler Center for Pain Control, 2901 Wilshire Blvd. Suite 345, Santa Monica, CA 90403.)

Imagination in Sports

Visualization is even used in sports. Australian psychologist Alan Richardson reported in the *Research Quarterly* the effects of visualization on the free-throw scores of basketball players. Three groups of students were chosen at random, none of whom had ever practiced visualization. The first group practiced making free throws every day for twenty days. The second group of students made free throws on the first and twentieth days, with no practice in between. The last group also made free throws on the first and last days. But in addition to this they spent twenty minutes a day imagining sinking baskets. In their minds, if they missed the shot, they tried to correct their aim on the next shot.

The first group who practiced free throws each day improved 24 percent between the first and the last day. The second group who only practiced on the first and last days made no improvement. The third group who visualized shooting free throws improved 23 percent. Numerous other studies involving dart throwing and other athletic activities show the same type of results.[4]

Research also concludes that mental practice is more effective if the visualizer "feels" as well as "sees" the activity he is symbolically practicing. The person visualizing the free throw will have better results if he "feels" the ball in his hands, "sees" the ball drop through the basket and "hears" the ball bounce. Using all the senses creates a greater sense of reality to the experience and provides more dramatic results.

Racketball and tennis players spend time prior to important

matches visualizing their shots hitting in a specific spot. To be effective, their visualization action must be very detailed. W. Timothy Gallwey, in his book *The Inner Game of Tennis,* tells tennis players to:

> . . . Stand on the base line, breathe deeply a few times and relax. Look at the can (a tennis ball container placed in the backhand corner of one of the service courts). Then visualize the path of the ball from your racket to the can. See the ball hitting the can right on the label. If you like, shut your eyes and imagine yourself serving and the ball hitting the can. Do this several times. If in your imagination the ball misses the can, that's all right, repeat the image a few times until the ball hits the target. Now, take no thought of how you should hit the ball. Don't try to hit the target. Ask your body . . . to do whatever is necessary to hit the can, then let it do it. Exercise no control; correct for no imagined bad habits. Having programmed yourself with the desired flight of the ball, simply trust your body to do it. When you toss the ball up, focus your attention on its seams, then let the serve serve itself.[5]

Relieving Anxiety Through Imagery

Imagery is something most of us use to some degree every day, sometimes in a negative way. Have you ever started the day out irritated over something your spouse did or said to you? During the day you dwelt on it, visualizing what you were going to do and say when you next saw your spouse. When he or she made an appearance you were ready with an articulate, well-rehearsed description of the offense and your displeasure! Your spouse was probably amazed at the refinement of your presentation! It was actually nothing to be amazed at, for you had prepared well. What if you were to take that same effort and energy and put it to use in a highly constructive positive direction?

Let's look at some real-life situations in which imaging can help you. Suppose you feel concerned about giving a speech.

The following exercise is called a role-rehearsal run and is designed to supplant the negative visualization behind the worried feelings.

Sit or lie down. Make yourself comfortable. Close your eyes. Breathe in and out slowly and deeply. Allow yourself to relax. Deepen this relaxation by whichever technique works best for you. Go to a level where you can visualize, where images flow freely and easily. Allow an image to come to mind of a meeting room where you have been asked to give a talk. Picture yourself in the front of the room. Look across the room. Notice details—the color of walls, where the door is and what it's made of. Notice the windows and pictures on the walls. Now look at the chairs; notice how they are arranged and what they are made of. Look at the people. Notice the kinds of clothes they are wearing. See if you recognize any friends or colleagues in the group. Now imagine walking over to a table or lectern to begin your talk. Notice what the table is made of, put your hands on it and feel it. Take a few deep breaths until you feel calm, clear and relaxed. Listen as the people in the audience quiet down. Allow the quietness to enter you and make you calm. See the people looking at you in a friendly, interested way. Now hear yourself begin the lecture. Your voice is clear and loud enough for everyone to hear. Your speech is organized, interesting, and conveys exactly what you wish to say. As you're speaking, you feel increasingly confident and comfortable. You can tell from the looks on their faces that the people in the audience have understood what you've said and are stimulated by it. As you end the lecture you hear excited talk begin among members of the audience. A number of people come up to you with stimulating questions and you answer them readily.[6]

In this exercise, your goal, while giving a presentation, is to feel at ease and have the audience enjoy it. You can apply the same type of visualization if you are fearful about preparing dinner for company, going to the doctor, and so on. Change the details to fit your own situation. It is important that you

"rehearse" the situation again and again. The repetition allows
you to make changes in your words or actions and refine them.
The more you visualize yourself succeeding, the more likely
you are to succeed.

An additional way to relieve the anxiety over an impending
situation is not only to visualize yourself accomplishing the
task successfully, but also envision yourself several days,
weeks, and months after the event. This enables you to see
yourself beyond the moments of anxiety and concern.

Imaging to Free You From Your Past

Imaging is a gift from God. The use of our imagination is the
use of an act of creation. Imagination is to our emotions what
music is to a ballad. It is our internal eye creating pictures as
real and vivid as those outside us. We use our imagination to
re-image past and to pre-image future. We run movies in our
minds.

Who do you see as the director and producer of these
movies? Is it someone from your past, who still lives within
you? Or is it a cooperative venture between yourself and the
Lord? You need Him to assist you because your imagination
was damaged in the Fall. The first time the word *imagination*
was used in the Scripture it was depicted as something evil.
"The Lord saw that the wickedness of man was great in
the earth, and that every imagination and intention of all human thinking was only evil continually" (Genesis 6:5 AMP).
Because of the Fall, our imaginations can be distorted and
misused.

We can choose what we image about, but there are also
images that uncontrollably pop into our minds from the past
or from our subconscious. The images we evaluate as wrong,
immoral, or sinful make us feel uncomfortable or guilty.
I shouldn't think that, we say to ourselves. *That's terrible. I
must not have those thoughts as a Christian.* Often we repress those images, instead of dealing directly with them,

and then they surface again at a later time. Depending upon the intensity of the images, they may even continue affecting us.

What does Scripture say? Are we to push evil thoughts into our subconscious or get rid of them entirely?

If you have an unpleasant image about someone in the past, maybe even from your childhood, the apostle Paul tells you to "let all bitterness, and wrath, and anger, and clamour, and evil speaking, be put away from you, with all malice: And be ye kind one to another, tenderhearted, forgiving one another, even as God for Christ's sake hath forgiven you" (Ephesians 4:31, 32). If you are tormented by impure thoughts, you should ". . . consider the members of your earthly body as dead to immorality, impurity, passion, evil desire, and greed, which amounts to idolatry. For it is on account of these things that the wrath of God will come, and in them you also once walked, when you were living in them. But now you also, put them all aside: anger, wrath, malice, slander, and abusive speech from your mouth" (Colossians 3:5–8 NAS).

Sometimes we try to hide our imagination or thoughts from God, but that is futile. Instead of presenting our complete selves to Christ we offer Him a hypocritical mask. He wants us to be honest with Him and share the truth about ourselves. He knows what we are thinking anyway, but He waits for us to take that step of transparent honesty, which is an indication of both our trust and our dependence upon Him. Since it is His nature to help, He wants to give us what we need.

How can we get rid of bad thoughts or images? We can't by ourselves. Without assistance we do not have the capability to extract these images from our minds. Colossians 3:15 states, "And let the peace of Christ rule in your hearts . . ." (NAS). The person of Jesus Christ is the answer. Jesus wants us to be open and honest about our thoughts and images. Instead of repressing our thoughts and condemning ourselves for them, we should bring them to Christ. By honestly sharing them with

Him, we give Him the opportunity to cleanse our minds of the images that may be dominating us.

But we must *want* to let go of these images. The real issue in the area of change is desire or motivation. We must come to the place where we can say to God, "I do not want to have these images and thoughts. They have created a barrier between me and others and between me and You. I want the thoughts and images You have for me. Help me to use my imagination and thought life in such a way that I can grow, mature, help others more, and bring glory to You!"

Begin by first praying for the desire to be rid of these thoughts. Invite Jesus Christ into your thought life. Ask Him to send the Holy Spirit into the depths of your imagination, to stir up those buried thoughts that are still affecting you. It is safe to do this in the presence of Jesus Christ and with His strength and comfort. As an image or thought surfaces that you desire to give to Christ, in your mind see yourself actually taking it and handing it to Him.

Some people find it helpful as they pray to lift one hand to their heads, place the thought in that hand, and then reach forward and place it in Jesus' outstretched hands. The physical movement, along with the prayer, has a greater sense of reality to it and strengthens their motivation. This type of praying takes time and often needs to be repeated for each image or thought that emerges. This is not to say that these thoughts will never return, but hopefully you are now willing to face them and deal with them in a positive way. The old proverb says that you can't stop the birds from flying over your head, but you can stop them from building a nest in your hair. The prophet Isaiah assures us that God "will keep him in perfect peace whose mind or imagination is stayed on him" (*see* Isaiah 26:3).

In this age of mechanization, as we have become more and more enamored with gadgets and computers, we have lost some of the use of our imaginations. Remember what it was like as a child to lie in the backyard, in the grass, and see castles form in the clouds? Remember the games you created, with imaginary people and cars that were very real to you? Imagery is being able to use God's gift to dream, visualize, and create. We need to ask Him for clearness of thought and direction, so that we do not neglect this God-given power that is available to help bring about change in our lives.

Imaging to Bring a Sense of Peace

You can bring a greater sense of peace and calmness into your life through imaging. Begin with your physical body. Disconnect the phone. Find the most comfortable chair or couch in your office or home, settle back, and close your eyes. This is a time to sag. Relax your muscles starting with your toes. Stretch out your legs. Then flex your ankles, straighten out your toes as though you were pushing them right off your feet. Now, relax. Let your head relax and roll back. Roll it around so your neck muscles become loose. Let each hand flop on your knee. Feel it resting there limply and gently like a soft feather. Begin to open your eyes, but imagine that each eyelid has an invisible weight on it slowly pulling it closed again. Now imagine the gentle hand of Jesus lightly touching your face and smoothing the tension away. If there is a frown on your face, let it evaporate. Picture the tension leaving your face, your arms, your torso, your legs, your entire body. You feel calm and peaceful and relaxed.

Now that your body is relaxed, begin to relax your mind. This takes concentrated imagination. See yourself alone at the inlet of a beautiful lake among the pines and aspens. It is the morning of a clear, cloudless day, and the sun is creeping across the mountain. All around you is a forest of trees, flowers, and wildlife. You are sitting on a soft spot in the ground, with your back against a tree. You feel the bark through your shirt and smell the freshness of the air. You are taking in the sounds of the wildlife and the wind in the trees.

Your sense of smell awakens to the aroma of your surroundings. Vivid paintbrush and columbine flowers are interspersed amongst the trees. The treetops sway in the gentle breeze. A squirrel races overhead from tree to tree, and a stationary chipmunk gazes at you. The light of the morning slowly makes its way down the mountainside into the forest and then brilliantly reflects off the smooth surface of the water. The lake is a mirror of the blue sky, broken only when a trout jumps after an insect. The ripples on the water are tight at first and then slowly expand outward until they once more become part of the flat surface of the lake.

The warmth of the sun feels so nice upon your face. It is like a benediction of God's creation, saying that it is complete and good and here for you to enjoy. Birds call to one another, and you feel relaxed and at peace with yourself and with God. The tension in your body fades away until it is gone. You are experiencing one of the joys of life that God wants you to know. In the midst of the turbulence of life, there is a calmness just like the peace and calm in the eye of a hurricane. This is His promise. Experience this calmness now as you reflect upon His word. "Yea, though I walk through the valley of the shadow of death, I will fear no evil: for thou art with me; thy rod and thy staff they comfort me" (Psalms 23:4).

"Let not your heart be troubled: ye believe in God, believe also in me. In my Father's house are many mansions ..." (John 14:1, 2). "Thou wilt keep him in perfect peace, whose mind [or imagination] is stayed on thee ..." (Isaiah 26:3). If God were speaking these words directly to you, what tone of voice would He be using? What expression would be on His face? Sense the love and concern coming from the One who is giving you these promises.

God made masterpieces when He created us. We were made in the image of God, just a little lower than the angels. The perfection of God's creation was marred at the Fall, and sin is ever with us. But God gave us His Son to take care of the problem of sin and to give us a new relationship with Him. His presence breaks us free from the paralysis of sin and frees us to use our imaginations for His glory!

How better could we glorify Him than by putting our imaginations to good purpose, using them as a powerful tool for refashioning our lives. Through imagination we can store up grievances or set aside all hurts and resentments. How much more profitable it is to do the second than the first!

Relinquishing Your Resentments

One of the greatest hindrances to making peace with your past is harboring resentments. A resentment is a feeling of hurt or anger, often caused by a real past experience or the continuation of a past experience.

Sally, a twenty-seven-year-old housewife showed her resentment when she said, "I've never been so insulted in my life; I'm crushed! I called my parents today, and again all I got was criticism and anger. Just once, I would like a pleasant conversation. I'm tired of talking to them and coming away wounded and bleeding. I wish I could make them feel the way I do."

Bill, an engineer with an aerospace company, fumed, "I'm so mad. My boss doesn't know what a compliment is! He never notices what I do, and last week he took one of my suggestions and made it his own idea. Guess who got all the credit!"

And Kathy, who has been married for a year now, tearfully said, "My husband is so insensitive. I'm not sure he realizes what marriage is all about. Demands and crude remarks are his fortes! Just wait until the next time he wants to get cozy!"

Every one of these people has been offended. It has happened to you before, and it will probably happen again. Altercations, differences, and offenses frequently occur between individuals, families, groups, and nations. Apologies, clarification of issues, armistices, and peace treaties make it possible for people and nations to live their lives unhindered and unaffected by the other. But does peace really occur? Does a resolution of differences really take place? Is there peace and harmony or is there a lingering resentment?

Nations often agree to stop their hostilities and killing and sign a peace treaty. But that doesn't necessarily stop the warlike attitudes. Years after the World War I armistice, resentment seethed and eventually fanned the flames of World War II.

Even though a governor may issue a pardon to a prisoner, which in effect says he has paid his debt to society and there is no further penalty—the record is clear—resentment may still remain in the prisoner.

Your spouse or parent may apologize and even give you a gift to show his or her good intentions. And you say, "Oh, that's all right. Let's just forget it happened." But inwardly you still feel cold and unforgiving.

Harboring unresolved resentments is another indication of the child within you. In your past there were significant individuals or groups whom you feel ignored you, belittled, abandoned, or in some way attacked you. Keeping them always in mind restricts you and breeds resentment. But you may have buried some of the memories in your subconscious mind. Then one day you discover that one of them comes out unexpectedly, when you encounter a person or a situation that resembles the past experience.

Stuffing hurt feelings and unresolved conflicts into the subconscious is common, but it keeps them alive. How can you tell if inner resentments are lingering beneath the surface of your memory?

1. You feel like striking back or telling off those in authority.
2. You explode for no apparent or obvious reason.
3. You engage in a power struggle with your spouse and view him or her as your enemy.
4. You avoid or fear any type of contact with your parents.

5. You compare yourself with other family members. You either feel inferior to them or you compete with them.
6. You make caustic or spiteful comments toward those you love.
7. You feel unappreciated or left out at work/or at home.
8. You experience somatic complaints which could include stomachaches, headaches, backaches, and so on.
9. Your outlook on life itself is basically pessimistic or negative.
10. You feel restricted in the expression of emotions toward others, even those with whom you have a "close" relationship.
11. You feel your family never really cared for you or that you were mistreated in some way by them.

Now just because you have one or more of those symptoms does not necessarily mean that you still feel resentment. You may have already resolved and worked through your feelings. But so many people have not!

Do You Want to Let Go?

The first step in relinquishing resentments is to become aware of them and identify them. This is not always the easiest thing to do. The second step is to forgive yourself for who and what you are now and to forgive the significant people of your past for what they did and for who they are.

"Yes, I already know this. I know I should do it, and it would be best for me! But how in the world do I do this? And honestly, there are times when I guess part of me doesn't want to let them off scot-free! I waver back and forth. What do I do?" This was the cry of a client who for years had never felt free to live her own life. Her struggle is similar to many others with the same inner dilemma.

The question you have to ask yourself is, *Do I want to let go of my resentments, or do I want revenge?* What is your honest answer to this question? It is not possible to get rid of these feelings if you are still seeking a bit of revenge.

Lewis Smedes described it well when he said, "Nobody seems to be born with much talent for forgiving. We all need to learn from scratch, and the learning almost always runs against the grain."[1]

Many of us live with one foot on the road of wanting to forgive and the other on the road to wanting revenge. We are immobilized. Why not make a commitment one way or the other? Why divide your energy? Why be halfhearted?

If the part of you that wants revenge is stronger than the forgiving part of you, then how are you going to get revenge? Does the other person know that you resent him? Is he aware of your craving for some sort of vengeance? Have you written out your plan of vengeance, with specific details of what you plan to do? Have you bluntly told this person about your feelings and your specific plan to get back at him? If not, why not? If revenge is what you want, why not get it over with and free yourself so your life can be full and unrestricted?

Your reaction is probably, "What a ridiculous idea! How could you suggest such a radical and unbiblical idea? I would never want to do that, and even if I wanted to, I couldn't do it." Really? If that is true, then why not give up your resentment completely and be washed clean of your resentful feelings?

If you forgive that significant person from your past, it means you will change your response from distrust and resentment to that of love. Love frees you to disagree with what another person says or does without becoming resentful. It even gives you the freedom to determine how much you are involved in that person's life. You can learn to communicate in an honest way and not be hooked into old patterns. The change in your attitude may help the other person change. And if it doesn't, the person may choose to back off from your relationship when he discovers you can no longer be pushed and manipulated.

Giving up your resentments may also involve your giving up:

1. Having someone to blame for the predicaments or situations you are in.
2. Feeling sorry for yourself.
3. Talking so much about the other person or your past.

Resentment means you have given that other person control of your emotional state. You have shifted the power source to someone else. Why give the power source to a human being? Instead, give it to the person of Jesus Christ and allow Him to work in your life.

There is a saying that "what you resist persists." This means if you are unwilling to let loose of the past, especially resentment, get set for a repeat performance in some other way. Your emotional upset will reappear in some other form. For example, if the person you resent is a parent, are you aware that some of the following may occur:

1. The marriage partner you choose for some strange reason begins to resemble the parent you resent.
2. You begin, in time, to act like the parent you never wanted to be like. You behave like that parent in time and begin to treat others in a similar manner as your parent treated you.
3. You may even find that you experience some of the same illness or emotional upheavals your parent experienced.

I have seen all these characteristics emerge in the various people whom I work with in counseling. Fighting painful memories and bitterness takes a lot of energy. Because of this energy drain, people tend to respond to other people in one of two ways: Because of fear, they become hesitant to respond to others with openness and intimacy; or they may be so starved for love, affection, and acceptance that their response is *too* open. They soon find themselves in great difficulty because of the desperation surrounding their search for acceptance and love.

How to Resolve Resentments

There are numerous ways to overcome and release resentment. In my own counseling I use an approach that incorporates some of the better techniques currently practiced by therapists.[2] These suggestions can be effective whether the person you resent is still living or is deceased. Begin by completing the following steps, in writing.

First, list all the resentments you have toward the particular person you are allowing to continue to limit your life. List each hurt or pain you recall in as much detail as possible. Write out exactly what happened and how you felt then and feel now.

One client shared the following list of resentments:

> I feel hurt that you made sarcastic remarks about me in front of others.
> I feel piqued that you found it hard to ever give me approval.
> I resent that you wouldn't listen to me.

Another client shared:

> I hate the fact that you called me trash and treated me the same.
> I resent the fact that you ran around on my dad and made me carry that secret as well.
> I feel offended by the way you try to use me for your own benefit.
> I can't stand manipulation of my life even today.
> I resent you not loving me for who I am.
> I feel indignant the fact that I am messing up my life today because of wanting to prove to you I'm no darn good, just as you said I was.
> I resent you and all women.

Please be aware that you may experience considerable emotional upheaval as you make your list. Other old, buried feelings may surface at this time, and you may feel upset for a while. Prior to and during this writing ask God to reveal to you the hidden and deep pools of memory, so your inner container can be emptied. Thank Him that it is all right for you to wade through and expel these feelings at this time. See Jesus Christ in the room with you, smiling and giving His approval of what you are doing. He is saying to you, "I want you to be cleansed and free. No longer do you have to be lame, blind, or deaf because of what happened to you."

Don't show these lists to anyone else.

Second, after writing as many resentments as possible, stop and rest for a while. By doing this you may be able to recall others you need to share. You will probably not remember every one, and you do not need to.

Third, upon completion of the writing, go into a room with two chairs. Imagine the other person sitting there and accepting what you are verbally sharing with him. Take your time, look at the chair as if the person were there, and begin reading your list. At first you may feel awkward and even embarrassed. But these feelings will pass. You may find yourself amplifying what you have written as you share your list.

Next, after you have read your list of grievances, sit back, relax, and imagine this person responding to you in a positive manner. In your mind see him saying to you, "I want to hear what you have to share with me, and I will accept it. Please go ahead and tell me. I need to hear what you have to say."

Imagine the person you resent actually hearing you, nodding in acceptance, and understanding your feelings. You may find yourself becoming very intense, angry, depressed, anxious, and so on. Share how you are feeling with that imagined person. Remember, not only is that other person giving you permission to share all of your present and past feelings, Jesus is there, also giving you that permission. You may find that sharing and talking about just one resentment will be enough for you to handle at one time. If you find yourself emotionally drained, then it is important to stop and rest and relax. After you have done this, you can resume your normal tasks for the day. At another time you will continue to share your list of resentments.

Finally before you conclude your time of sharing, close your eyes and visualize you, the other person, and Jesus standing together with your hands on one another's shoulders. Spend several minutes visualizing this scene. You may wish to imagine the resented person verbally accepting what you have said to him.

Once you have completed all the steps, you may find that you will need to repeat them several times, over a period of weeks, until the past is purely a historical memory. If there is more than one person involved, you will need to complete these steps with each one.

Another helpful method is to write a letter to the resented person. Be sure that you do not actually give this letter to the individual in mind. For some, the written sharing may be more helpful than the verbal.

Start your letter as you would any letter: Dear _____. This is not an exercise in style or neatness or proper punctuation. You are simply identifying, expressing, and draining your feelings. At first it may be difficult, but as you begin you will feel the words and feelings flowing. Do not hold back! Let out all the feelings that have been churning underneath. This is not a time to evaluate whether the feelings are good or bad, right or wrong. They are there and need to be drained. Once the letter is complete, you may need to rest from this experience.

As I work with clients in therapy, and have them write such a letter, I ask them to bring it to their next session with me. Often they hand me the letter as they enter the room. "No," I say, "I'd like you to keep the letter, and we will use it in a little while." At the appropriate time I ask them to read the letter aloud. Since there is an empty chair in the room, I ask them to imagine that the resented person is sitting in the other chair, listening to the reading of this letter.

I remember one client who wrote a very extensive letter and was surprised when I asked her to read it in my presence. During the first fifteen minutes of reading this letter to her mother, the client was also crying and tearful. But during the last five minutes, the crying ceased, and there was a positive bright lilt to her voice as she concluded her letter. Through this experience the issues of her past had definitely been changed.

I have found that it is important to share this letter with a highly trusted person. This can be a friend, a spouse, or a relative. The person should be someone who will listen and be supportive, not make value judgments or violate your confidence. Sit across from your friend and share your letter with him. You may also want to use this approach with your list of resentments, but only after you have shared them as previously described.

The other person can make comments, but only those that support you in what you are sharing and encourage you to share more. The person is not there to comfort you or be sympathetic, but to be *for* you. The experience of sharing this in the presence of a caring person can be very healing. Be sure to thank this friend for listening.

Give a Positive Response

There is one final step that is a very necessary part of the process. Not only is giving up resentment important; it is also essential that you project a positive response toward the individual who wronged you. This positive response can be love, acceptance, friendliness, and so on. It would be impossible just to exist in a state of neutrality, with neither negative nor positive feelings. I have had a number of clients state that they feel nothing. Their feelings are neither positive nor negative. They are blasé. But what they have actually developed is a state of emotional insulation toward the other person. And insulation usually means a blockage of some sort.

This last step is a means of finding any resistance toward the development of some sort of a positive response. It is a way to eliminate the last holdout of resentment.

Take a blank sheet of paper. Put the resented person's name at the top of the page. Then underneath the name write it again, but this time use the salutation approach from a letter. "Dear _____"

Under the salutation, write "I forgive you for . . ." and complete the sentence with whatever has bothered you for all these years. For example, a person might write, "Dear Mother, I forgive you for always trying to control my life."

Next, stop to capture the immediate thought that comes to mind after writing your "I forgive you for . . ." statement. Does that thought contradict the concept of forgiveness? Do you have a rebuttal or protest of some kind? Is there any anger, doubt, or caustic feeling that goes counter to your desire to forgive? Write these contradictory thoughts immediately beneath your "I forgive you for . . ." statement. Don't be discouraged if your protests or contradictions are so firm or vehement that it seems you have not done any forgiving at all. *Continue the exercise* and write out the same "I forgive you . . ." statement, followed by your immediate thoughts, which may still be contradictory.

Keep repeating this process until the pockets of resentment and resistance have been drained. You will know you have reached that point when you can write your "I forgive you for . . ." statement and can think of no more contradictions or resentful responses.

Some people finish this exercise with only a few contradictory responses. Others have a great deal of resentment and use several pages. Following is a typical example of how a young man worked through his resentments toward his father, for the father's anger toward him and rejection of him during his growing-up years. Notice how his protests and contradictions become progressively less intense and his resentment drains away to the place where he can simply say, "I forgive you for your anger toward me and your rejection of me," and feel no further need for rebuttal.

Dear Dad:
I forgive you for your anger toward me and your rejection of me.
(*I guess I really don't yet.*)
I forgive you for your anger toward me and rejection of me.
(*I still don't feel your love and your acceptance.*)
I forgive you for your anger toward me and rejection of me.
(*I wish you would be friendly when I call.*)
I forgive you for your anger toward me and your rejection of me.
(*I would like to, I guess.*)
I forgive you for your anger toward me and your rejection of me.
(*I wish you could be different. How has Mom handled you all these years?*)
I forgive you for your anger toward me and your rejection of me.
(*I am afraid of trying to build a better relationship with you.*)
I forgive you for your anger toward me and your rejection of me.
(*I do have feelings of love for you, but I don't want to be rejected if I tell you.*)
I forgive you for your anger toward me and your rejection of me.
(*I feel less resentful now as I do this.*)
I forgive you for your anger toward me and your rejection of me.
(*I am tired of protecting myself from you and of the hurt I feel when I try.*)
I forgive you for your anger toward me and your rejection of me.
(*I wonder what happened to you when you were growing up to make you the way you are. I wish you would tell me. I*

guess I have never asked you, either. Would you tell me?)
I forgive you for your anger toward me and your rejection
of me.
(*I think I am learning to.*)
I forgive you for your anger toward me and your rejection
of me.

After you have completed your own version of this exercise, sit
in one of the two chairs described earlier. Visualize the resented person sitting in the other chair, accepting your forgiveness and telling you so. Take as long as you need for this step,
because it is very important. Later, destroy your list of statements. It is important that you show this list to no one. Burn it
or tear it into tiny bits as a symbol that "... old things are
passed away; behold, all things are become new" (2 Corinthians 5:17).

Responding to Your Parents in a Childish Way

Sometimes your own honest emotions frighten you. You feel
they are wrong, and you shock yourself when you face them.
And of course there is that old nemesis called guilt. When pain
and frustration exist between you and your parents, some of
these "radical" feelings burst forth. You may have such trauma
that on occasion you wish that your parents had never existed.
Who needs that amount of pain? You may also feel that if your
parents were not your parents you would probably have nothing to do with them. You certainly would never select them for
friends or even associate with them. You may feel like having
nothing to do with them again. And on occasion you make that
resolve and then break it.

But perhaps there is a better way. Perhaps there is a positive
way of becoming unstuck from the past.

It's hard work to abandon a model you have spent years

building, "But until the model is superseded by a compassion-ate model, you are still stuck."[3]

Your biggest job is to quit responding to your parent as you did when you were a child. It would be nice if your parent would learn to do the same toward you, but you are responsible for your reactions, and your parent is responsible for his or hers. How do you quit responding in a childish way? Recognize when you are replaying old response patterns with your parent, and pull the plug on that old recording. Don't view your parents as bad or maliciously evil for the way they responded to you. Blame is not what you are trying to establish.

Sometimes people wonder why they have so much difficulty forgiving another person. You are what you are today because of your early experiences. You're a combination of your memories and your present events. Resentment tendencies usually have their roots in memories of the past, some forgotten and some conscious. Many of the experiences of your childhood will affect the ease or difficulty you have in forgiving.

Let's review for a moment our early life history.

An infant is totally dependent upon his mother for physical and emotional survival. Usually the child's mother conveys love and security, through touch, feeding, warmth, and so on. Through this the small child learns to trust others. When the child is frustrated, upset, crying, and unhappy, mother is loving and faithful. This develops a sense of trust in the child.

But if the child's cries are usually ignored or responded to with irritation, the child learns that mother and others cannot be trusted. The child feels confused because he starts to feel what it means to be unappreciated and neglected, but he does not understand why this is happening to him. What he does learn is that the world is unloving and unwelcome. This type of start in life teaches a child to mistrust others. He learns that they cannot be depended upon.

Feeling unappreciated and neglected creates a low tolerance level for frustration in the child. When his needs are not responded to, he can easily become angry and frustrated. This also can create a predisposition to depression when the child becomes an adult. It is the germination ground for strong feelings of resentment and hostility and creates the beginnings of his withholding forgiveness toward others. A child may not understand why his or her feelings are so strong, but he does begin to feel "I am not loved." Because of his frustration and resentment, he is unable to forgive others for his plight.

Have you ever considered the price you pay when you are alienated from your parents? An incomplete and strained relationship is costly, but how often do we make an audit to discover our losses?

Instead we learn to wear protective armor, so that recurring feelings of hurt and rejection are deadened. Our defenses, however, do not eliminate these feelings, for they are still alive and warring within us. We may love our parents but also not be able to stand them.

What is your relationship with your parents? What are your feelings about them? What will your answers to the following questions reveal?

1. Do you have any regrets or resentments from your childhood? If so, what are they?
2. When you are with your parents, do you feel relaxed and enjoy yourself?
3. When you are angry, is it ever because of a resentment or unresolved hurt from the past?
4. Do you confide in your parents, and do you trust them?
5. Do you need to forgive something your parents did in the past? if so, what is it? Can you forgive them without trying to change them?
6. How comfortable do you feel in taking care of your parents as they age?
7. Describe the type of love and acceptance you feel from your parents. What specifically do they do to indicate to you that they love and accept you? If you feel unloved and rejected, what is this based upon?

8. If your parents are deceased, do you still have resentments or regrets toward them at this time?

As you listen to the inner messages you have carried over from your childhood, which would you like to change? Write your answers to the following questions on a piece of paper.

1. Why am I following this inner voice or compulsion?
2. Does responding in this way make any sense to me? Is it really logical or healthy? Is it just an automatic response carried over from before?
3. What are the consequences of continuing this way?
4. What are the consequences of not continuing this way?
5. If I make a change at this time, will anyone be hurt? If so, why?
6. Will a change make my life better or worse?
7. What is my motivation for making a change? Is it out of vengeance, to rebel, or because I feel it is best?
8. Will there be any disapproval from anyone for this change? Can I handle the reactions? Is it my own disapproval I am most concerned about or someone else's? What can I do to accept this change?
9. Have I invited God into this decision to change? How can I ask His assistance in making the change a reality?

Your emotional binds to the past may be to a person or to a deeply entrenched inner message. It is easier to be emotionally free if our parents encouraged us to grow toward independence. If you had parents who wanted you to remain weak, dependent, and somewhat ineffectual, they were probably responding toward you from their own inner child. You may be more tied in than you believe. And there may be some security in being emotionally bound, because, even though it is detrimental to us, it is familiar; and it can be scary to cut loose. In fact, cutting loose can be risky if you have not yet established a new source of security. But cutting loose is part of growth.

Are you still emotionally dependent? Answer these questions to find out.

1. Do you still live with your parents? If so, why?
2. Do you still live near them? If so, why?
3. How do you feel about the amount of contact you have with your parents? on the phone? through letters? in person?
4. How would you feel if you were to have less contact with them?
5. Do you involve them in your life as much as you want, not enough, or too much?
6. In what way have you become a parent to them? What do you do for them that they used to do for themselves? How did this situation come about? What are your feelings about this?
7. Have you avoided becoming more independent? What are the risks of independence?
8. If you do something that goes against your parents' wishes for you, what happens?
9. What is it your parents expect from you at this point in your life? How do you know?
10. What would happen if you chose not to be with your parents on Thanksgiving or Christmas? What would they feel and say? How would you feel?
11. What do you do to gain their approval? How do you feel when you have their disapproval?[4]

The Cost of Making Peace

The mixed feelings you have toward your parents can positively affect your health, your work, and especially your marriage. Many marriages deteriorate and end because of the unresolved hurts and rejections in one or both partners toward their parents.

But there is also risk in making peace. What might you have to give up in order to make peace with your past? Have you concentrated upon the cost or the benefits? You may need to give up anger, your resentments, your need to punish, your need to blame.

You may need to accept the fact that love, approval, or acceptance is there and has been there all this time. You may need to accept the fact that love, approval, or acceptance will never be there.

Many of us move through life never having our needs for approval, acceptance, or recognition met by our parents. And we never will. No other person can make up in a few days or even months what we feel we lacked for years and years. To continue to strive to meet parental expectations or to rail against their lack of love is futile. The solution is to come to the place where we can say, "It's all right for this to have occurred. It was painful, but I can go on in my life without the influence of the past. It is okay for them to be them and for me to become all that I can."

Joyce Landorf has written *Irregular People,* one of the most insightful books of our time on this topic. An irregular person is a very significant person to us, possibly a sibling or a parent, who is emotionally blind to us and cannot give us what we feel we need from him or her. The irregular person continues to wound us, reinforcing some of the negative messages we've already incorporated into our life. The affirmation we want will not be coming.

In her book, Joyce shares a letter she received from Dr. James Dobson concerning her irregular person. He writes:

> Joyce, I am more convinced every day that a great portion of our adult effort is invested in the quest for that which was *unreachable* in childhood.
>
> The more painful the early void, the more we are motivated to fill it later in life. Your irregular person never met the needs that he should have satisfied earlier in your life, and I think you are still hoping he will miraculously be-

come what he never has been. Therefore, he constantly disappoints you—hurts you and rejects you.

I think you will be less vulnerable to pain when you accept the fact that he cannot, nor will he ever, provide the love and empathy and interest that he should. It is not easy to insulate yourself in this way . . . but it hurts less to expect nothing than to hope in vain.

I would guess that your irregular person's own childhood experiences account for his emotional peculiarities, and can perhaps be viewed as his own unique handicap. If he were blind, you would love him despite his lack of vision. In a sense, he is emotionally "blind." He's blind to your needs. He's unaware of the hurts behind the incidents and the disinterest in your accomplishments, and now Rick's wedding. His handicap makes it impossible for him to perceive your feelings and anticipation. If you can accept him as a man with a permanent handicap—one which was probably caused when *he* was vulnerable—you will shield yourself from the ice pick of his rejection.[5]

From *Irregular People* by Joyce Landorf, copyright © 1982, pp. 61–62, used by permission of Word Books, Publisher, Waco, Texas 76796.

Here is part of the answer to freeing us up so that we don't become an irregular person to someone else. The first step is to accept this person as he or she is and not expect the person to change.

Second, remember that this person has probably experienced the same negative treatment at some point in his life. Now you have the opportunity to break the cycle. The Bible says: "Remember ye not the former things, neither consider the things of old. Behold, I will do a new thing; now it shall spring forth; shall ye not know it? I will even make a way in the wilderness, and rivers in the desert" (Isaiah 43:18, 19).

Lloyd Ogilvie suggests:

The sure sign that we have an authentic relationship with God is that we believe more in the future than in the past.

The past can be neither a source of confidence nor a con-
demnation. God graciously divided our life into days and
years so that we could let go of yesterdays and anticipate
our tomorrows. For the past mistakes, He offers forgiveness and an ability to forget. For our tomorrows, He gives
us the gift of expectation and excitement.[6]

One of our problems is that most of us have a better memory
than God does. We cling to our hurts and nurse them, which
causes us to experience difficulty with others. We actually play
God when we refuse to forgive others or ourselves. When we
don't forgive, it not only fractures our relationship with others
but with God as well.

Is it fair to be stuck to a painful past? Is it fair to be
walloped again and again by the same old hurt? Vengeance is having a videotape planted in your soul that
cannot be turned off. It plays the painful scene over and
over again inside your mind. It hooks you into its instant
replays. And each time it replays, you feel the clap of pain
again. Is it fair?
Forgiving turns off the videotape of pained memory.
Forgiving sets you free. Forgiving is the only way to stop
the cycle of unfair pain turning in your memory.[7]

Can you accept your parents for who they are, what they
may have done, and for the messages they gave you? This
means forgiving to the point where you no longer allow what
has occurred in the past to influence you anymore. Only by
doing this can you be free—free to develop yourself, to experience life, to communicate in a new way, free to love yourself
and your spouse.
Lloyd Ogilvie asks the question:

Who's your burden? Whom do you carry emotionally,
in memory, or in conscience? Who causes you difficult reactions of guilt, fear, frustrations, or anger? That person
belongs to God. He's carrying him or her too, you know!
Isn't it about time to take the load off, face the unresolved
dynamics of the relationship and forgive and forget?[8]

Perhaps Webster's definition of *forget* can give you some insight into the attitude and response you can choose. Forget means "to lose the remembrance of . . . to treat with inattention or disregard . . . to disregard intentionally; overlook; to cease remembering or noticing . . . to fail to become mindful at the proper time." Is there someone in your life who is suffering from emotional malnutrition because of resentment and unforgiveness?

Not forgiving means inflicting inner torment upon ourselves. When we reinforce those parental messages, we make ourselves miserable and ineffective. Forgiveness is saying, "It is all right, it is over. I no longer resent you nor see you as an enemy. I love you, even if you cannot love me back."

> When you forgive someone for hurting you, you perform spiritual surgery inside your soul; you cut away the wrong that was done to you so that you can see your "enemy" through the magic eyes that can heal your soul. Detach that person from the hurt and let it go, the way children open their hands and let a trapped butterfly go free.
>
> Then invite that person back into your mind, fresh, as if a piece of history between you had been erased, its grip on your memory broken. Reverse the seemingly irreversible flow of pain within you.[9]

We are able to forgive because God has forgiven us. He has given us a beautiful model of forgiveness. Allowing God's forgiveness to permeate our lives and renew us is the first step toward wholeness.

6

Coping With Rejection

Before you can make peace with your past, you have to cope with rejection, which is the feeling of not being loved or wanted by another person. You feel cut off, isolated, and often lonely. You feel disconnected, like an island with no land mass to connect you to the mainland.

> It is difficult to feel at home in the world if you have never felt at home in your own home. If you were rejected as a child, you have an extreme emotional handicap; you are, in effect, the original person "without a country."
>
> You may see yourself as an outlaw, unacceptable to yourself and to others. Your self-depreciation is bitter and you feel, almost automatically, bitterness toward others that leads you often to distort the attitudes of others.[1]

Do you sometimes feel like an outlaw fleeing from the bounty hunters? Who is it that is after you? Is it other people? Or are you really chasing yourself? Is it others who turn their backs on you? Or do you slam the door in your own face?

The more important the rejecter is to you, the more severe the feeling. Rejection can be an occasional experience or a constant one. Many people grow up from childhood with the belief that acceptance and affection have a price tag—they are not free gifts, but something one earns by accomplishing something or attaining some goal or by refraining from doing something.

During childhood one man never felt free to make any noise or disruption at home. Noise was absolutely forbidden. When friends came over to see him, he would become embarrassed if they were loud or noisy in front of his parents. Today, as an adult, he rarely experiences any peace or feels relaxed. He is constantly edgy. Because of his parents' restriction against noise, he interpreted this to mean that they did not appreciate him. He also remembers feeling that he was never "good" enough. Even though he may not have actually been rejected by his parents, he felt that he was.

Rejection communicates to you that you are not worth having a relationship with or even knowing. True rejection is rare. What you perceive as rejection may be simple neglect or negative responses such as anger or rage. True rejection means that you are not accepted at all and are treated as if you are a burden or millstone wrapped around your parents' or another person's neck. A child who is rejected may be injured by the rejecter or given away to someone else. And of course this does happen. But usually rejection takes more subtle forms.

If rejection occurs to any degree, we feel hurt and even bitter. The hurt remains with us, and we become very sensitive to actual or apparent rebuffs. Such a person anticipates rejection and reads it into other people's responses. He assumes the worst to begin with and is very suspicious. It is difficult to be open with some people, for showing true feelings may lead to their experiencing another painful rejection.

We also tend to reject ourselves if we feel we were rejected by someone we cared for. We treat ourselves like criminals and end up directing more criticism and disapproval toward ourselves than our parents or others ever gave us. Do you cheer yourself on in life, or do you make disapproving and rejecting comments to yourself? Are you a worse critic than others? Do you ever say, "You're too sensitive"? "You won't succeed"? "You're not worth loving"? You may be rejecting yourself if you do. How do you parent yourself?

Part of your inner struggle, however, may focus around some unanswered questions. You may feel guilty or somehow responsible for your parents' rejection of you. And, if so, you may have feelings of worthlessness that contribute to your continuing suspiciousness. What then could others see in you? Why would they want to be involved with you? And if this is so, you may have developed a protective armor, like a porcupine, to ward off others' involvement.

If you received rejection as a child, rather than feeling love, you may have felt puzzled. You saw other parents giving their child love and acceptance. Why were you not receiving love, too?

Why Are Children Rejected?

Parental rejection of children in our society is by no means uncommon. What are the reasons? Do mothers and fathers reject their children for the same reasons? Perhaps we are influenced by the prevailing attitude of our society. We are creatures of our time and culture, as Alvin Toffler has observed in his book *Future Shock*. We live in a throw-away society. Our relationships with people, places, and things tend to be temporary and fragile. We see this in the lack of desire on the part of married couples to commit themselves to anything or anyone for a lifetime.

Why do parents reject their children? Some just plain dislike the child. Whether it be his looks or his personality, they just do not care for him. Some children are rejected because of some apparent defect, such as a low IQ or because another child who entered the home is more attractive or gifted. In some cases, if a child too closely resembles a parent who loathes himself, it is easy for that parent to project those feelings of dislike onto the child. Children who resemble the other side of the family may receive the fallout of stored-up hostility. This anger may be directed against the spouse or even against the spouse's parents. If a child is the result of an untimely pregnancy he may experience rejection. The child is seen as a continual interference. Unfortunately some parents have a child because they don't know how not to have one. Some parents want to have a child of a certain sex, and they reject the child born with the wrong gender.

Sometimes a child may start out feeling a high degree of affection from one or both parents, but after a time begins to experience rejection. He may gradually realize the affection he is receiving from one or both parents is not genuine. This is because, in the beginning, he was actually a stand-in for the other parent. For example, a mother who does not have a good relationship with her husband may transfer her affection to her infant, because the child cannot reject either her or the attention she gives. And as an infant he can also give back some acceptance and affection. But as he grows older she no longer considers him a safe recipient of love. He has stopped being a safe replacement for her spouse, so she begins to withdraw her acceptance and affection. This gives the child the message that he has never really been loved for himself.

Mothers reject their children for various reasons. Some associate the child with his father. In the eyes of the mother, the child is the father, and to the extent that the father is hated, the child is hated. The child's own identity is denied because of her strong negative feelings toward his father.

Other mothers find it easier to reject the child than to run the emotional risk of losing the child. Still others feel that a child is the bind that keeps the couple stuck in a bad marriage. The degree of problems in the marriage may influence the amount of rejection toward the child. If the husband was not as attractive as the wife desired, or if she is abused by him, her rejection could be extreme, because she feels locked into the marriage.

If a marriage is shaky, and the wife believes that a child will save the marriage, the child may receive conditional acceptance. When the marriage fails to improve because of the presence of the child, that child may be blamed for the failure. The mother may feel she is now stuck with a child as well as a husband.

There are some mothers who resent their children because

they feel they have to share their husband with the child. The child is seen as a competitor for the attention and affection of the father. An illustration of this is the wife who is waiting for her husband's return home each evening, but before she can greet him, her four-year-old daughter runs around her and leaps into her daddy's arms. He responds with warmth and affection to his daughter for a minute or two and then turns to greet his wife for a few seconds. The woman's resentment grows each day.

During the past ten or twenty years, more and more women report a new feeling. They feel their child has deprived them either of the job they once had or the job and career they would like to have. Their resentment centers around being forced to stay at home just to care for a child. This to them is limiting and unfulfilling. As they talk to other women who also feel stuck at home and to women who are enjoying their jobs their resentment grows. They feel they are being held captive!

What about fathers? What are some of the reasons why they reject their own children? Some of the motives are the same as for the mothers—an unhappy marriage, an unattractive child (for whatever reason), the wrong time for a pregnancy, and so on.

There are, however, some additional reasons why fathers reject their children. Some fathers feel personally inadequate for the job. Being a breadwinner, husband, and father is both threatening and overwhelming. The child is seen as a burden and thus is not given love and affection. Also, a child becomes a ball and chain to the father who feels that he made a wrong choice in the woman he married.

But even if you were rejected as a child, it is possible to overcome the results of this rejection.

How Do You Handle Rejection?

If you were rejected as a child, is it necessary for you to go through life with emotional wounds? Listen to these words of hope for the present and the future:

Being unloved by a parent may always leave scars, but the wound can be healed and healthy growth can begin anew. It is worth giving up even those songs and dances that have helped you to survive parental unlovingness because there are better ways to feel okay. In exchanging the old songs and dances for more authentic movement, it is crucial to begin to accept that your parents' not loving you is a statement about them and not about you. In other words, it bespeaks a defect in their ability to love rather than a defect in your lovability. It becomes particularly important to see the child within your parent because it is the inner child, too big a part of your parent, that made him or her unable to love you. If your parent had you to please his own parents, or his spouse, or society, then it was the little child in him trying to be the good, conforming child, trying to get approval or avoid disapproval, that made the decision. You were brought into this world by a child, and children can only play at being loving parents.[2]

How do we handle rejection? A rejected person soon learns to use defense mechanisms to protect himself and to conceal the fact that he has been rejected. These mechanisms are psychological tricks he plays upon himself to lessen the pain. It hurts to admit he has been rejected. It makes him feel that he is somehow inferior. What are these defense mechanisms? Let's look at some of the more common ones.

Some people use the defense mechanism of *repression*. They force the truth of rejection below their level of awareness and shackle it there. But the feelings of being rejected still tend to influence much of their behavior. Repression is a subtle form of denial to protect us from the bare truth. But the feelings have been buried alive and will someday crawl from their grave.

Rationalization is a defense mechanism many of us use. As one man put it, "It wasn't that my parents rejected me; they just didn't need me as much." We try to explain away the rejection. We may say, "Well, Dad was so busy trying to make a living for us it was impossible for him to spend time with me or my brother. He showed his love by providing for us. We always had plenty to eat, and every other week he would give us a toy or model plane. Parents have a lot of responsibilities, you know." Others say their parents were too sick, didn't have any training in how to be parents, or that they showed their love in other ways.

Some people use *regression* to protect themselves from the pain of rejection. They revert to patterns of living that actually belong to childhood, instead of operating on an adult level. An adult child who has been rejected moves away from home and gains some independence. But if for some reason he is forced to move back home, he finds the parent who once rejected him now loving and accepting. Now the adult child is caught between the horns of a dilemma. He values the freedom and independence he has when he is away from home. But he also values the love and acceptance he finds when he moves back home. So he decides to stay at home. He feels that the trade-off of his freedom for his parent's love and acceptance is not too high a price to pay. But in actuality he is being prevented from assuming adult roles.

Some people *insulate themselves* to avoid the pain of rejection. They build walls around themselves to avoid the trauma and hurt. One man told me that emotionally he turned himself off to his parents at the age of twelve. He just blocked out whatever they did or said. He was numb when it came to emotional input or response. Others block out their past life but also refuse to anticipate the future. They live a day at a time, just in the present. Today is all that matters. It is safer that way.

Still others of us use *reaction formation.* Instead of insulating ourselves from the pain of rejection, we reach out to our parents and smother them with love. We may feel a need to repay our parents for all they have done for us, or we want to be the sole provider for the parents who rejected us—to the amazement of other people. Some adult children even put the welfare of their parents ahead of their own families. Giving to our parents over and above the call of duty enables us to deny our feelings of rejection and prevents us from giving in to the sub-conscious desire to reject them back.

The most common response to rejection is to find approval no matter the cost!

How Does Rejection Affect a Marriage?

If you are a rejected person, you entered marriage starved for love and acceptance. If you married a rejected person, you married a starving person. If you both were rejected, watch out! Your expectations and demands in one another will lead you to heights of frustration, anger, and disappointment.

But once in a married relationship, the rejected person's need for attention, acceptance, and affection is constant. This puts a great burden on his partner. When the spouse is unable to respond at times with the same intensity of affection the rejected person expects, the person feels rejected again. He may then become depressed, angry, or hurt and make even more demands on his mate for love and acceptance.

If a rejected person constantly questions his partner's love for him, trouble is on the horizon. After a while the partner will become fed up with being doubted and say, "You can believe what you want to believe. Either you take what I say at face value, or you don't. I don't have any other way of convincing you, and I am sick and tired of trying. I give up!" Of course, this will just create more seeming rejection, even though the partner's frustration is certainly justified. People do not like to have their word doubted or to have their love constantly tested. When such a situation continues for a long period of time, the partner becomes angry. No matter what he does, it is not enough.

Some rejected people actually seek out a marriage partner who will repeat what they experienced as a child. They are familiar and comfortable with the same kind of distance and mistreatment they experienced for so many years. Then if the rejecter-type partners never show approval or acceptance, the rejected ones relive their old familiar pattern. They don't realize that they will never gain acceptance from someone who, because of his own inadequacies and deficiencies, has little or nothing to give. It is like going to a dry well for water.

Overcoming Rejection

To overcome the effects of rejection, we must begin with ourselves and the person of Jesus Christ. We cannot base our solution to this deficit on an outside resource such as a friend or a spouse. Eventually someone else may be able to help us, but we must first of all find the Source of acceptance who will fulfill all of our needs. This Source, in the person of Jesus Christ, is not built upon the whims and lacks of another struggling person.

After seeking guidance and strength from Jesus Christ, why not begin by recalling those experiences of acceptance and approval you did receive as a child that you are overlooking? They were there! Your selective memory needs to be switched over to a new channel.

Can you recall specific times when you experienced trust, love, acceptance, and hope? Perhaps you, like the children of Israel, need to be called back to positive memories. Moses reminded the people to "... remember all the ways which the Lord your God has led you in the wilderness. ... Therefore, you shall keep the commandments of the Lord your God, to walk in His ways and to fear Him" (Deuteronomy 8:2, 6 NAS). Isaiah urged the people to "remember the former things long past. For I am God, and there is no other ... like Me" (Isaiah 46:9 NAS).

Remembering who we are in the sight of God can, in time, become a stronger force, overshadowing the negative memories from the past. God asks us to remember, to refocus our attention, to challenge our negative way of responding to life and correct it. How is this done?

First, *change the direction of your thought life and remembrances.* "Be anxious for nothing, but in everything by prayer and supplication with thanksgiving let your requests be made known to God. And the peace of God, which surpasses all comprehension, shall guard your hearts and your minds in Christ Jesus. Finally, brethren, whatever is true, whatever is honorable, whatever is right, whatever is pure, whatever is lovely, whatever is of good repute, if there is any excellence and if anything worthy of praise, let your mind dwell on these things" (Philippians 4:6–8 NAS).

Second, *identify your parental attitudes and your present reaction to them.*

Third, *identify the rejecting comments you make to yourself and challenge them.* Your own self-belittlement and self-criticism keep the past alive and vibrant.

Fourth, if you are seeking approval, as you see yourself trying a little too hard, *force yourself to stop sooner.* Lower your expectations and reduce your efforts to please. Realize that you have already been approved by God and begin responding in that way. Recall the values and worth you have because of God's view of you.

Fifth, commit yourself to *treat yourself in a new, positive way* and not as you have treated yourself in the past.

The more we incorporate the biblical perspective of ourselves into our consciousness, the easier it will become to overcome hurtful memories and crippling messages. For it is God who does it in us.

Who are we? How does God see us? He sees us as being worth the precious blood of Jesus.

> Or do you not know that your body is a temple of the Holy Spirit who is in you, whom you have from God, and that you are not your own? For you have been bought with a price: therefore glorify God in your body.
> 1 Corinthians 6:19, 20 NAS

> Knowing that you were not redeemed with perishable things like silver or gold from your futile way of life inherited from your forefathers, but with precious blood as of a lamb unblemished and spotless, the blood of Christ.
> 1 Peter 1:18, 19 NAS

> And they sang a new song, saying, "Worthy art Thou to

take the book, and to break its seals; for Thou wast slain, and didst purchase for God with Thy blood men from every tribe and tongue and people and nation."

Revelation 5:9 NAS

God knows us through and through! He is fully aware of us. "And the Lord said to Moses, '. . . you have found favor in My sight, and I have known you by name.' " (Exodus 33:17 NAS). "Before I formed you in the womb I knew you, And before you were born I consecrated you . . ." (Jeremiah 1:5 NAS). "I am the good shepherd; and I know My own, and My own know Me, . . . and I lay down My life for the sheep. . . . My sheep hear My voice, and I know them . . . and they shall never perish . . ." (John 10:14, 15, 27, 28).

Dr. James Packer writes:

> There is tremendous relief in knowing that His love to me is utterly realistic, based at every point on prior knowledge of the worst about me, so that no discovery now can disillusion him about me, in the way I am so often disillusioned about myself, and quench His determination to bless me. . . . He wants me as His friend, and desires to be my friend, and has given His Son to die for me in order to realize this purpose.[3]

The times in our lives when we are at peace with ourselves, not bound by the past, are the times when we feel as though we belong. We feel wanted, desired, accepted, enjoyed. We feel worthy: "I count." "I am good." We also feel competent: "I can do it."

These feelings are essential, for they work together to give us our sense of identity. But the times of feeling complete may be all too infrequent. Now is the time to remember our roots, our heritage. We are created in the image of God. He wants His work to be complete in us. When we relate to His Son Jesus Christ by faith, we have the potential for a sense of inner wholeness (*see* Colossians 2:10).

This then, is the wonder of the Christian message: that God is this kind of God; that He loves me with a love that is not turned off by my sins, my failures, my inadequacies, my insignificance. I am not a stranger in a terrifying universe. I am not an anomalous disease crawling on the face of an insignificant speck in the vast emptiness of space. I am not a nameless insect waiting to be crushed by an impersonal boot. I am not a miserable offender cowering under the glare of an angry deity. I am a man beloved by God Himself. I have touched the very heart of the universe, and have found His name to be love. And that love has reached me, not because I have merited God's favor, not because I have anything to boast about, but because of what He is, and because of what Christ has done for me in the Father's name. And I can believe this about God (and therefore about myself) because Christ has come from the Father, and has revealed by His teaching, by His life, by His death, by His very person that this is what God is like: He is "full of grace."[4]

Finding Parental Approval

For some of us, finding parental approval is quite impossible, because that parent is deceased or is unable to give us this gift. But the fact remains that we never outgrow our need for an accepting parent. We even parent ourselves sometimes to help fulfill this need. But is that enough? No. However, realizing that God is our heavenly *Father*—the kind of father a father should be—can give us deep emotional satisfaction.

We read, ". . . He [the Father] hath made us accepted in the beloved [Christ]" (Ephesians 1:6). We did absolutely nothing to earn that acceptance; we submitted to Him, and He made us accepted to Himself! "For God so loved the world, that he gave his only begotten Son . . ." (John 3:16). He made us accepted because He loved us!

He is pleased to call us His sons. That gives us a position

with Him in His family. We know we are somebody to God; we have been redeemed from being a nobody! In our relationship with the Son of God, we are assured of worthiness. Being forgiven all sin, we lose our sense of guilt and the associated feelings of being a nobody, a bad person.

We also have a secure sense of competence as we relate to the Holy Spirit as our Comforter, Guide, and Source of strength. He is with us daily to face our situations with us, and He is in sovereign control of the situations that He allows us to experience.

He imparts the ability to live a godly life and maintain a relationship with God, in spite of the undertow of habit and the emotional insecurities we derived from our childhoods. He is our competence, making it possible to live the Christian life and hold onto the sense of being somebody in God.[5]

This is the beginning for new growth: new memories, new messages to ourselves, new self-talk, new outward communication, and new relationships. It is possible!

Why not act upon the biblical truths and release your hurt child of the past? Can you treat yourself in the same manner in which God sees and accepts you? Allowing the rejected child in you to live your life for you is not helping you find what you really want. By accepting yourself as worthy and lovable, you can also give up your desires to hurt and strike back at others.

If you were rejected by your parents, the problem was not within you but within them. So many parents who did this were rejected themselves in some way, but they never found a way nor took the time to work out their own difficulties. They just directed them onto you. Are you directing your rejection onto any others in addition to yourself? Perhaps the rejection occurred because your parents were not ready to be parents—they were immature. Most people can conceive and give birth to a child, but that is the easiest part of all. Living with that child, loving that child, and meeting that child's needs does not come naturally. Your parents may have had a deficiency in their capacity or desire to be loving and caring. Parenting takes depth of character, maturity, wisdom, and patience. Perhaps these were absent.

Give your parents permission in your mind to have their own expectations of you. Say to yourself, "It would be nice to have my parents' approval, but it is not earth shattering if I don't get it. I have God's approval, others' approval, and my own approval. I won't be perfect, and I don't have to be perfect. God has taken care of that for me with the gift of His Son."

Make a list of the expectations that you and your parents have for each other.

1. List your parents' expectations of you in order for them to accept you.
2. List your expectations of yourself. Which of these are yours and which are coming from other people?
3. List your expectations for your parents.
4. Which of the expectations listed in number 1 have you discussed with your parents? Have you ever gone to them and shared with them your feelings of not being accepted? With some parents this is possible, and with others it is not. You will have to decide.

Continuing to play the role of a rejected child carries a high price tag. Be sure that you have expressed your anger and resentment as I suggested earlier. Give up your fantasy of having your parents change. If your parents are unhappy, the roots of their unhappiness did not lie with you but in their own past. You can never make up for what your parents did not receive in their childhood. You cannot undo what has been done to them or to yourself in relationship to them. You *can*, however, live your own life for yourself and allow the presence of Jesus Christ to be the fulfilling source.

Do not open and reopen wounds from your past by behaving as you used to with your parents. Look for acceptance, approval, and love from those who have the capability of giving love. This would include being loving to yourself.

Embrace Yourself With Love

You may wonder how you can begin to feel loving and accepting of yourself when you have no memories of parental acceptance and love toward you. Have you no memory of early loving responses from your parents? Probably not. Our memories become selective, and the painful ones that may be frequent tend to erase the positive memories. But you can embrace yourself with love. Here is a suggestion that has helped a number of people.

Take your photo album and look for pictures of you as a young child. As you look through these pictures do not concentrate on any hurts or rejections that may arise from your bed of memories. Rather, concentrate and draw up pleasant experiences. Think of those events and interchanges in which others gave love, acceptance, and praise to you. Think of times when you were loved.

Now close the book and just visualize a photograph of yourself as a child. Picture yourself as that child in a corner of the room. Become that child and feel what the child is feeling and experience what he or she needs. In your mind go over to that child, pick up, and put him or her on your lap. Tell that child everything you think that child wants and needs to hear.

Dr. Howard Halpern tells of two experiences that illustrate how to embrace yourself with love.

> A man in his forties, who felt his father never loved him, sat his little boy self on his knee and said, "You're a fine kid. You're fun and warm and sensitive. And I'll teach you how to be strong and how to fight because you'll need lots of strength and self-confidence. I'll teach you not to be afraid to reach for what you want. I can do this for you because I love you and want you to be strong and able and happy. Let me give you my love." As he was telling this to himself as the child on his knee, he was discovering what the child in him wanted from his father and didn't get, and he was learning how he can now give more of this to himself. And a depressed, suicidal, self-deprecating woman of

about thirty who felt that both of her parents were cold and unloving held her little girl self in her arms and, tears flowing, told her, "Oh, my darling little girl. You're really so kind that I even like it when you're naughty. Don't be frightened and don't be shy. Be strong and stand up for yourself. Because I'll tell you a secret: You're just the little girl I always wanted, that I always dreamed of having, and I'm so glad you're here and alive." She was letting herself feel what the child in her so desperately wanted and never received, and she was learning how to be nurturing to that child or, more simply, learning to be good for herself.[6]

As you picture your own experience visualize the person of Jesus Christ standing there with one hand on your shoulder and one hand on the shoulder of the child. As you complete what you are saying to the child hear Him say, "I want you both to know that I love each of you unconditionally. Because of this, you have the capacity to love yourself and even love others who have been unloving to you."

What you are actually doing is reparenting. And the excitement about this is that you can become more of a loving parent to yourself than others have been. Allow yourself to love you.

Your parents have given you love according to the ability that they had at the time. Please remember that. They have not had the opportunity to reparent themselves. It would be helpful for you to understand their inner child if possible. How much do you really know of their childhood? What were the traumas, traditions, family conflicts, family experiences that make your parents the way they are? What were their hardships, socially or economically? What was their view of Christianity, and how strict or lenient were their parents and church? Do you know? If not, and if your parents are alive, could you discuss these questions with them?

If you can't get the answers directly from your parents, aunts and uncles can fill in the gaps. Recently I received a 300-page book from my uncle, which had been run off on a small press. He had decided in his seventies to write a book about his boyhood experiences on the farm in Iowa. Because my mother was close to him in age, much of what he wrote about included her. His description of life on the farm, the economic struggles, the hard work, and family traditions was very interesting. Gaps in my knowledge and lost information now came to light, which helped me better understand my mother.

Look at the images of your parents as children. Try to discover their feelings as children. How were they controlled? What were their pressures and insecurities? What were they taught about being a man or a woman? What do you feel are their unresolved conflicts? What are their true feelings about their own parents?

Look for a photo of your parents as children with the rest of their families. Can you determine anything from that family photo? What were their expressions, their body language? Were they sitting or standing? How did your parents relate to their siblings? Were they loving, warm, cold, distant, competitive, accepting, supporting? How have the losses of family members affected your parents? The losses would include death, divorce, a child leaving home, and so on. In the photograph how do your parents seem to relate to others? Are they relaxed, stiff, smiling, at ease, touching others? Now look for photographs of your parents' wedding and the early years of their marriage. What were their hopes and dreams when they first married? What were and what are the needs of your parents today?

Understanding some of your parents' problems may help you break free and live your own life. It is too bad they treated you the way they did, but will you continue to allow yourself to live with the image they have assigned to you? Can you live free, in the image that God has given to you? You are worthy and have been declared to be worthy.

Reparenting Yourself

Now the process of reparenting your inner beliefs about yourself can begin. You are worthwhile, and you probably do not give yourself credit for your worthwhile actions.

Make a list of the positive acts you do. Give yourself credit for acting in a healthy and positive manner. Don't pay attention to your lacks and defects. We all have them, and some can be corrected in time. Some cannot. Compliment and thank yourself for who you are at this time in your life. Have you ever said to yourself, *Well, I am going to thank me for what I did today. And I can do this because those behaviors were positive and worthwhile. I know that God has been with me, helping me express my value and worth to myself and to others.*

That may sound strange to you. But I wonder how you would feel if you committed yourself to doing that very thing each day for a month.

You will need to reach out to others to develop close relationships. If you will begin to relinquish your porcupine coat and become a risk taker, you will find that others will probably respond in an even more positive manner than before. (Many of them have responded positively to you, but it has been hard for you to see it because of the suspicious filter in your mind.)

You will need to open yourself to others, slowly and confidently. Do this even though you have mixed feelings or perhaps do not feel like doing it at all. Lower your expectations of others, for they, too, are human. If you expect 100 percent performance and total acceptance, you will be disappointed. Other people have the right to disagree and even become a bit upset with you, but that does not mean they are rejecting you or disliking you. You, too, have the right to be upset with yourself and not reject you. It's possible. We are not rejected people. We are accepted. Try living your life as an accepted, not a rejected, person. It's well worth the effort.

7

Breaking Away From Perfectionism

Most of us would like to be successful. Some of us, however, turn success into a requirement. When this happens, we become preoccupied with the pursuit, not of excellence, but of perfection. The greater the degree of pursuit, the more often our joy is lessened. Perfectionism becomes a mental monster.

In order to prove that they are good enough, perfectionists strive to do the impossible. They set lofty goals and see no reason why they should not achieve them. But soon they are overwhelmed by the arduous task they have set for themselves. The standards of a perfectionist are so high no one could consistently attain them. They are beyond reach and beyond reason. The strain of reaching is continual, but the goals are impossible. Their worth, they think, is determined by attaining these goals.

As we discussed in chapter 2, perfectionists usually are the result of a home where children had to prove their worth before they could feel accepted by their parents. This character trait is one more that needs to be brought into focus if you are to make peace with your past.

The Treadmill of Perfectionism

Marie's home was a showcase. The furnishings, the decor, the magazines, every item was perfectly arranged. The drapes were evenly hung without the slightest sag. Each picture was placed at the same height, to the exact inch. Nothing was irregular in this house—except perhaps the woman whose perfectionism was evident in her surroundings. She constantly drove herself and the other members of the family in order to maintain order and an immaculate house.

Marie paid meticulous attention to the details and was very precise in everything she did, but it was never enough. She always felt her home "could be better," and she underrated whatever she did. Whenever guests showered her with compliments, she beamed at the time, but the satisfaction never lasted. *It could be better!* she would say to herself. She appeared successful in creating an attractive home, but actually she felt more like a "successful failure."

Unfortunately, the amount of time Marie spent maintaining this showcase was out of proportion to the result. She was a perfectionist. Her standards were too high. Very possibly her parents' standards were high also and she had been programmed to be a perfectionist.

Perfectionism is a thief. It offers rewards but it actually steals joy and satisfaction. In Marie's mind an old and worn tape was playing over and over again: *That isn't good enough. If you do better, you might receive some approval. Try harder. But don't make a mistake.* She was on a treadmill that never stopped. When she compared herself to other people, guess who came out in second place?

When we require perfection of ourselves, we assign our life to a set of rules. These often come in the form of "I must," "I should," "I ought to." From the minute we are born, we are surrounded by advice, warnings, *shoulds,* cautions, and directives. But some of the urgent *shoulds* that are born in our childhood later grow into anxious striving for today's and tomorrow's perfection. The drive to be perfect brings with it a strange bedfellow—a very high sensitivity to failure. The pain of failure or doing less than one's best is much more acute for the perfectionist because of the height of his standards. The greater the distance between performance and standards, the higher the degree of pain.

How Does a Perfectionist Think?

Perfectionism is not so much a type of behavior as it is an attitude or a belief. Let's climb inside the head of a perfectionist and discover some of his beliefs.

One such belief is that *mediocrity breeds contempt.* The thought of being ordinary is intolerable. Even the garden planted or the lunch served must be the best. Perfectionists have to have the best sex, the best grammar and speech, the best behaved children, the best communication in marriage, the best dishes. The standards they set for other family members are unbearable and frequently cause discouragement. The perfectionist is not really competing with other people, but reacting to the inner message *You can do better.*

Often the perfectionist tends to do *all or nothing.* "Either I go on a diet all the way or not at all." "Either I learn racketball and become expert, or I don't learn it at all." If he begins a project or activity, the first time he is unable to continue, the perfect pattern is broken, and he gives up completely. The all-or-nothing belief is a difficult way to measure progress.

Another belief is that *excellence comes without effort.* If a person really is an outstanding individual, even difficult tasks should come easily. A person should be able to catch on instantly, make the right decisions on the spot. Notice the word *should,* for it is a constant companion. And if the plan does not unfold according to his beliefs, procrastination sets in at once.

Another belief is the importance of *going it alone.* It is a sign of weakness to delegate or ask for assistance. He must do it all himself and not ask for advice or opinions. The perfectionist tends to work and suffer alone, and when he cannot complete the task, he delays it. A perfectionist lives with the fear of appearing foolish, inadequate, or of not knowing what to do. Thus he hides his inner thoughts and feelings, especially those of fear and concern. He feels that other people will not accept his humanity, and this barrier robs him of the warmth of human contact.

A man once said to me, "What is left without my perfectionism? I would be average and inadequate. Who wants that? Not me. I'll keep on striving, because someday I'll get there. I do better when I push myself."

Another belief a perfectionist may have is that there is *one correct way to complete the task*. The main job is to discover that one right way. And until he has made that discovery, he may be hesitant to begin. Why make the wrong choice? This even keeps some individuals from committing themselves in marriage, for they certainly do not want to make the wrong selection.

A perfectionist usually *cannot stand to come in second*. This is an indication that he is competitive, but if you ask him, he will not admit to it. He dislikes losing so much that he tends to avoid activities that would involve direct competition with others. Instead he competes with himself. He does not want to compete and not come out on top. Some vary this principle slightly. They procrastinate to such an extent that failure is guaranteed. But they still hold the belief that they would have come out on top, if they had tried. This is a common protective device. Anything incomplete is still in the failure stage. Nothing is accomplished, for they do not believe in short-term goals. As one author put it:

> Perfectionists tend to think in absolute terms about what they do. In addition, they often think catastrophically; that is, they take one small event, such as a mistake, and exaggerate the consequences until the repercussions are staggering. They seem to react to one incident as if it were the beginning of the end, certain that devastation is just around the corner.

These catastrophic expectations are even more intimidating when they are nameless and vague, as they are in most people's minds. "My mind would be miserable if I weren't perfect," they moan. But in what specific ways would their lives be miserable? It is often both interesting and helpful for procrastinators to articulate the nameless fantasies of dread that haunt them. Ask yourself the question, "What would happen if I weren't perfect?" In addition to the general sense of doom you might feel at the thought of being less than exceptional, what specifics do you foresee? How bad would things get? What chain of events would lead up to the final castastrophe?[1]

The perfectionist lives by many unspoken rules. These are a powerful influence on his life. They also create tremendous stress. Here are some of the most common ones:

I must never make a mistake.
I must never fail.
I must play it safe so I always succeed.

An unspoken thought sequence for a perfectionist might go something like this: *I made a mistake. That's terrible. I must not make a mistake at any time. I've got to plan it out differently next time. If I make a mistake, I am not perfect. What will others think of me? They'll think I'm stupid and weak. Others have got to think highly of me. They shouldn't know my weaknesses. This is awful.* Such thinking invites stress, tension, procrastination, and even indecision.

These rules come from deeply held beliefs. If change is to take place, they must be repeatedly challenged.

If your rule is "I must always do my best," there is another rule behind it. That rule is "It would be terrible if I didn't do my best." A revision would be "I prefer to do my best, but it is all right not to be perfect. I feel better when I do my best, but I can learn to feel okay when I don't. In fact I can give myself permission not to do my best when that takes place."

Another rule to be challenged is "I must never make a mistake that others would see. I wouldn't be able to stand it if that occurred." A revision could be "I would prefer not to make mistakes in front of others, but it's not the end of the world. I can stand it. Other people are not as judgmental as I think they are."

What would your reaction be if you were approached by another person with the statement "Well, you certainly live in an average neighborhood, your house is quite average, and your car doesn't stand out. It's average, too. The way you dress is average. In fact, you are quite average. I really do not see you leading the pack in any area of life." How would you feel? Annoyed, insulted, angry, defensive, accepting, satisfied, sad, dejected, good? A perfectionist would be irate and possibly explode. Someone else might say, "Yes, I quite agree with you. I am satisfied with my efforts and my abilities and level of accomplishment. I feel good about myself and what has been attained. I enjoy life." But not a perfectionist.

A Perfectionist May Be a Procrastinator

The perfectionist has a need for certainty, not risk. He is comfortable about only those activities in which he is sure of the outcome. When the certainty is lacking, he can actually make himself sick by worrying over the right decision. He is afraid of failure, therefore he will not attempt to accomplish anything unless he is sure of success. So there are three possible ways he may react:

1. He will avoid working on those tasks he feels he will not be successful at accomplishing. Or he may work with a diligence and feverish intensity that affects those around him in a negative manner.
2. He may angrily object to questions or interruptions. His rigidity becomes encased in cement. His personality and responses become brittle.
3. He may wait until the last minute to begin a task that needs a great deal of time. This is actually a setup to provide him with a way out: "Well, of course I didn't do it

correctly. I didn't have time. I started too late to accomplish it." It was actually a semiplanned mismanagement of time. Procrastination is its name, and delay is its game!

Are you a delayer? Do you consistently put off doing tasks? Is your motto "Why do today what you can put off until tomorrow?" Now, not all procrastination is bad. We all face decisions and tasks that on occasion we consciously choose to delay. But a life-style of delays is another matter.

Why do people delay? We've discussed some of the reasons, but there are five more we need to consider.

1. Some individuals delay decisions or actions because of limitations. Physical medical problems make it difficult for them to move ahead.

2. Another reason for procrastination is ignorance of what needs to be done. The individual doesn't know what to do or that something needs to be done.

3. Strategy is another reason for procrastination. The businessman waits until the market is ripe before selling. He decides to postpone mailing a new advertisement, because research has indicated that January is a better month for a response. A woman delays making a trip to the store, because by doing it tomorrow she can take care of errands at three other stores in the same area.

These are delays we can all understand and accept. There is a good reason for each of them. But there are two other delays that are based more upon psychological difficulties than on solid reasons.

4. A fourth type of procrastination is that of the discomfort dodger. A task is put off because some parts of it make the person feel uncomfortable. This is not limited to unpleasant tasks but can include those which are basically enjoyable. If there are some hassles associated with it, the person feels "it just isn't worth it!"

The person may never have actually experienced the event or task, but the anticipated hassles are enough. He even has a tendency to expand the discomfort in his mind. If it takes thirty minutes to prepare to tackle a job, he sees it as taking an hour and a half. If it is snowing outside and he has to dress warmly in order to ski, he decides it is too cold to enjoy it. If it is twenty degrees outside, he sees it as ten degrees.

The more the person practices this type of delay, the more convinced he becomes that his perceptions are accurate. He even avoids small tasks, and an accumulation process begins. He may not only delay the event, but forget it as well, which brings about a whole multitude of consequences.

5. A fifth reason for procrastination is self-doubt. This is a changeable attitude that also involves self-depreciation and low self-esteem. He sees himself as lacking in some way. His faults loom out of proportion. This individual takes a look at his life, evaluates it, and comes up with a minus. He both imagines and cultivates his deficiencies: *If I am deficient and lacking, why try? Hey, I am not that stupid to try and end up with egg on my face.* This can be a conscious thought or an underlying thinking pattern. *Why try? I'll just end up proving that I can't do it! It's worse to experience the actual failure.*

The state of self-doubt is constant with some people, selective with others, depending upon the event, and fluctuates with others. It can be based on such things as mood, feelings, the situation, the environment, or who the people are in the individual's social group.

And then there are those who enjoy mixing their motives for procrastination. They put self-doubt and discomfort dodging together and have an extremely solid basis for procrastination.

If you are a perfectionist and are caught up in procrastination, what is it that you avoid? What are the areas or situations of life in which you procrastinate? If you are interested in getting rid of your desire to procrastinate, make a list of the areas of your life that you avoid or delay doing anything about. Take plenty of time in order to make the list as complete as possible. Now take an 8½-by-11-inch piece of paper and divide it into four sections. Title it "Accomplishment Inventory" (*see* figure 1). In the upper left section, list the tasks you usually put off in order of importance. In the upper right section, list the personal self-development tasks or activities that you delay, in order of importance.

Now take the bottom left section and do three things. Select one of the tasks from the section above and indicate a due date when it will be completed. Then write down what it is that has been stopping you from doing the job. Is it self-doubt or a desire to dodge discomfort? Finally, list three or four steps you will follow in order to accomplish your task. Do this with each task you have listed. Repeat this process with the personal self-development tasks you listed in the upper right section as well.

Having excessively high standards (being a perfectionist) is a sure way to invite depression into your life. Why? Because of the impossibility of being perfect in this life. It is as though you have two doors to walk through: one is marked PERFECTIONISM; the other is marked AVERAGE or even ABOVE AVERAGE. As you open the perfection door you run into a brick wall. Each brick is an obstacle preventing you from achieving perfection. The other door has no wall on the other side of it. Entering that door leads to growth and a balanced life.

A Perfectionist Cannot Be Perfect

Perfectionists are vulnerable to emotional turmoil, and they are not the highest achievers. They actually create self-defeating patterns of behavior, illogical and distorted thinking. They are successful failures.

The perfectionistic person is striving for adequacy. And therein lies the irony. The more we push for adequacy, the more it eludes us. The more we attempt to become adequate,

Accomplishment Inventory

Tasks I Put Off	Self-development Tasks I Put Off
1. Clean out the garage. 2. Answer correspondence. 3. Make arrangements for the next couples' party for church. 4. Replace muffler on car.	1. Lose fifteen pounds. 2. Spend one night a week with kids, learning about their lives. 3. Talk to my supervisor about a job evaluation.

1. *What I will complete and due date.*
I will sort through the twelve boxes in front of the car by next Sunday.
 	
2. *What's been stopping me?*
I don't like to do that work. I think it will take too much time. I don't know where to put it, and I don't know what my wife wants to keep or throw out.
 	
3. *Three steps I will take to accomplish this.*
  1. I will set aside three consecutive hours and work on this.
  2. I will sort one box at a time.
  3. Anything that has not been used for a year I will throw out.
	1. *What I will complete and due date.*
	I will lose fifteen pounds in the next three months.
	
	2. *What's been stopping me?*
	I enjoy eating. I don't really know what diet to go on. I'm not sure I can lose the weight. What if I lose it and I put it right back on again?
	
	3. *Three steps I will take to accomplish this.*
	  1. Call my doctor and the health spa for information on diet and exercise.
	  2. Talk to my wife about helping me with my diet.
	  3. Set up a chart to keep track of weight, food intake, and exercise.

Figure 1

the less adequate we become. Adequacy is a free gift to us and always has been. God has declared us to be adequate because of what He has done for us through Jesus Christ. Any shortage in our lives has been paid for by God's free gift. We can begin to express ourselves now out of our sense of adequacy, instead of striving to become adequate. We can let loose of the criterion of human performance, for God calls us to be faithful. This is the standard—faithfulness!

God's view of us is so much higher than anything we could earn or attain by our own efforts. Just look at these verses that prove my point:

> ... He chose us. ... to the praise of the glory of His grace, which He freely bestowed on us in the Beloved.
>
> Ephesians 1:4, 6 NAS
>
> And God created man in His own image, in the image of God He created him; male and female He created them.
>
> Genesis 1:27 NAS
>
> Yet Thou hast made him [man] a little lower than God, and dost crown him with glory and majesty!
>
> Psalms 8:5 NAS
>
> See how great a love the Father has bestowed upon us, that we should be called children of God; and such we are. ...
>
> 1 John 3:1 NAS
>
> Now to Him who is able to keep you from stumbling, and to make you stand in the presence of His glory blameless with great joy.
>
> Jude 24 NAS

We as believers are called to be perfect. But it is a call to continue to grow and mature. It does not mean never making an error or a mistake. It means looking at ourselves objectively, accepting and recognizing our strengths and talents, as well as areas of our life in which we are lacking. When we fail to live up to unrealistic standards, we create anger, depression, or both. When we are depressed, however, we feel like "I can't do anything right. Nothing works for me. I can't even be average." The best time to work on perfectionistic tendencies is not during our depression, but at a time when we can be objective about ourselves.

How can you break out of the straitjacket of perfectionism? First of all, reread the section in chapter 6 in which we discussed who you are from God's perspective. Reread that section each day and allow it to soak into your mind to counter all those other messages you have been listening to for years.

Following are some exercises to use if you would like to make a change. You probably won't have to do all these exercises before you experience change. Remember, you do not have to do *these* perfectly either!

1. Make a list of five to ten benefits of making mistakes. How do people grow and learn from them?
2. Imagine that you have been given an assignment to discuss why it is impossible for a human to be perfect. Write out a summary of what you would say.
3. Make a list of three of your recent successes and three of your failures. Aside from the effect upon your inner feelings, what else did each one of these accomplish?
4. List the techniques you use to keep yourself from failure. Would you be willing to tell three other people your plan for procrastination and avoidance? If not, why not?
5. Make a list of ten of your strengths. What other individuals are aware of these strengths?
6. Describe how God would see you if these ten strengths were not a part of your life.
7. Imagine yourself tackling some task and having it fail. Make a list of objective comforting remarks you could make to yourself at that time.
8. Each week admit some of your errors to a good friend.
9. How do you usually respond to someone who is having a difficult time at a task or who has failed? Write out what you could say to support and help him or her.
10. What is one task or activity that you are currently putting off because of your fear of failure? Make a commitment to complete that task soon. Identify what is the most difficult part of it and who you need to ask for assistance. What steps can you take to have an easier time with it? Break the task into small steps and set realistic goals.

11. What is your motivation for being a perfectionist? It may help to make a list of the advantages and disadvantages of perfectionism. You may discover (if you are honest) that the disadvantages actually outweigh the advantages. You may find that you are able to accomplish tasks but that you become tense, irritable, fearful of trying anything new, intolerant of others who do things differently, depressed when you fail, and so on.

   One man I was working with shared his list. The advantage of attempting to be perfect at work was that he got a tremendous amount of work done and received admiration from his superiors. But when he began to think about the disadvantages, he listed the following:

   > I am afraid of making a mistake, so I am on edge and irritable.
   > I am very critical of what I produce and waste time redoing the work.
   > I have the feeling that each job has to be better than the one before.
   > I find myself very critical of the mistakes of others. I guess they remind me of my fallibility.
   > I haven't produced much that is new in a long time. I am a bit hesitant to venture into a new area. It's the old fear "What if I make a mistake?"

12. One of the beliefs that you may have is that unless you aim for perfection you can never be happy. You can't enjoy life or have any satisfaction unless you attain your goal. Why not test this belief? Dr. David Burns suggests using an antiperfectionism form on which you record the actual amount of satisfaction you get from your activities. The activities could include eating a steak, mowing the lawn, fixing a broken toaster, preparing a talk, washing the car, and so on. Estimate how perfectly you did each task using a scale of 0 to 100, also, using the same scale, how satisfying each was. The purpose of this exercise is to show you that your satisfaction is *not* dependent upon being perfect. Figure 2 shows what a physician who believed that he had to be perfect listed.

Activity	Record How Effectively You Did this Between 0% and 100%	Record How Satisfying This Was Between 0% and 100%
Fix broken pipe in kitchen	20% (I took a long time and made a lot of mistakes.)	99% (I actually did it!)
Give lecture to medical school class	98% (I got a standing ovation.)	50% (I usually get a standing ovation—I wasn't particularly thrilled with my performance.)
Play tennis after work	60% (I lost the match but played okay.)	95% (Really felt good. Enjoyed the game and the exercise.)
Edit draft of my latest paper for one hour	75% (I stuck with it and corrected many errors, and smoothed out the sentences.)	15% (I kept telling myself it wasn't *the definitive paper* and felt quite frustrated.)
Talk to student about his career options	50% (I didn't do anything special. I just listened to him and offered a few obvious suggestions.)	90% (He really seemed to appreciate our talk, so I felt turned on.)

Figure 2[2]

I remember a college student I worked with many years ago, who was almost a compulsive perfectionist. He came from a home where you earned love by performing. If you attempted something and failed, then you received no love. Because of this, he developed a fear of failing. Obsessive thoughts interrupted his ability to concentrate. School failure was the worst for him. Thus, when he entered college he dropped out of school after the first four semesters, at final exam time, because he did not want to attempt the exams and fail. (Failure in his eyes was anything less than a strong A.)

For years this young man crippled himself with his perfectionism. Fortunately he received the help he needed through counseling. After he was married and working, he went back to college part time, willing to do his best and accept whatever he could accomplish. He got A's in his first twelve courses!

Fears of failure often enter our minds automatically. It is a part of our deeper-hidden self-talk that emerges from time to time as a means of hindering our lives.

Dr. Burns gives an example of a college student who was afraid of submitting a term paper because it had to be "just right." The student was given the suggestion to list his automatic thoughts and then identify the fear by using the vertical-arrow method. This approach is like peeling off the layers of an onion until the origins of the perfectionism are discovered. The process can be very enlightening as deeper fears, which have been covered over, are discovered. Fred's journey is shown in figure 3.

John Clarke once wrote: "We must stop being picture straighteners on the walls of life before we can find and bring joy in life."[3]

It's not so terrible to be average. In fact, the world is full of mostly average people. *Average* means we accept our strengths and weaknesses and do what we can to change the weak areas. As believers we are fortunate in that our attempts at growth are not in our own strength. We have at our disposal the resources of God. He calls us to be faithful, not perfect.

Automatic Thoughts	Rational Responses
1. I didn't do an excellent job on the paper. ⬇ "If that were true, why would it be a problem for me?"	1. All-or-nothing thinking. The paper is pretty good even though it's not perfect.
2. The professor will notice all the typos and the weak sections. ⬇ "And why would that be a problem?"	2. Mental filter. He probably will notice typos, but he'll read the whole paper. There are some fairly good sections.
3. He'll feel that I didn't care about it. ⬇ "Suppose he does. What then?"	3. Mind reading. I don't know that he will think this. If he did, it wouldn't be the end of the world. A lot of students don't care about their papers. Besides I *do* care about it, so if he thought this he'd be wrong.
4. I'll be letting him down. ⬇ "If that were true and he did feel that way, why would it be upsetting to me?"	4. All-or-nothing thinking; fortune teller error. I can't please everyone all the time. He's liked most of my work. If he does feel disappointed in this paper he can survive.
5. I'll get a D or an F on the paper. ⬇ "Suppose I did—what then?"	5. Emotional reasoning; fortune teller error. I *feel* this way because I'm upset. But I can't predict the future. I might get a B or a C, but a D or an F isn't very likely.
6. That would ruin my academic record. ⬇ "And then what would happen?"	6. All-or-nothing thinking; fortune teller error. Other people goof up at times, and it doesn't seem to ruin their lives. Why can't I goof up at times?
7. That would mean I wasn't the kind of student I was supposed to be. ⬇ "Why would that be upsetting to me?"	7. Should statement. Whoever laid down the rule I was "supposed" to be a certain way at all times? Who said I was predestined and morally obliged to live up to some particular standard?

Automatic Thoughts	Rational Responses
8. People will be angry with me. I'll be a failure. ♦ "And suppose they *were* angry and I *was* a failure? Why would that be so terrible?"	8. The fortune teller error. If someone is angry with me, it's their problem. I can't be pleasing people all the time—it's too exhausting. It makes my life a tense, constricted, rigid mess. Maybe I'd do better to set my own standards and risk someone's anger. If I fail at the paper, it certainly doesn't make me "A FAILURE."
9. Then I would be ostracized and alone. ♦ "And then what?"	9. The fortune teller error. *Everyone* won't ostracize me!
10. If I'm alone, I'm bound to be miserable.	10. Disqualifying positive data. Some of my happiest times have been when I'm alone. My "misery" has nothing to do with being alone, but comes from the fear of disapproval and from persecuting myself for not living up to perfectionistic standards.

Figure 3[4]

Figure 14–4 (pp. 310–311) in FEELING GOOD: The New Mood Therapy by David D. Burns, M.D. Copyright © 1980 by David D. Burns, M.D. By permission of William Morrow & Company.

8

Resisting Overcoercion

You are scanning the morning paper, and all at once an ad leaps out at you.

> Do you find it difficult to "get started"? Is your life bogged down by constant daydreaming? Do you just get your motor running and then turn it off? Do you find yourself tired much of the time? Do you feel that other people are to blame for your problems? Do you have lists and lists of things to do tomorrow, including doing what was on yesterday's list? If so, CONGRATULATIONS! You qualify for our organization! Just fill out the coupon with your name, address, and phone number, and we will send you your application immediately. You can become a member of our society with all of its privileges. Be sure to write today.

What a strange ad! It doesn't say what you are about to join! Perhaps you put the ad aside and say, "Well, that sounds like me, but I'll fill it out tomorrow and send it in." Then suddenly you realize you are doing exactly one of the things the ad asked about, so you say, "Maybe I better do this now. I'm curious to see what I'm applying for!" So you fill out the application, mail it in, and wait.

Days go by before there is a response. When the letter arrives, you slash the envelope open and see that it is an application to join the Society of Overcoerced Resisters!

"What are they talking about?" you fume. "Overcoerced Resisters, my foot! I'm no resister. I'm in charge of my life. I know what I'm doing. So what if I don't always accomplish what I'd like to?" You mutter and grumble, feeling disgusted, angry, and insulted. And why shouldn't you?

But then you glance at the application again and read this statement:

> You are probably upset by reading this application. You probably do not think that you belong in this organization. You may not. But, if you answered yes to several of the questions in the ad, my friend, you do belong! And if you would like to know more about being overcoerced, apply. If you would like to change your response to life, apply. Don't put it off until tomorrow. After all, if you belong in this club, your tendency will be to procrastinate, won't it?

All of a sudden you realize, "They're right. What have I got to lose? I guess I do belong."

In chapter 2 we talked about parental attitudes we experienced in our childhood, which still prevent us from walking on our own. One of these attitudes is overcoercion. A child who has been overcoerced relies too much on outside help. When he grows up, he still feels that he cannot do anything without direction from someone else.

Somewhere in your past another person attempted to direct, redirect, and control your life. This could have taken numerous forms, but often the coercer nagged and was anxious and pushy. His or her control over your life was all-consuming and left little or no opportunity for you to become your own person. You were unable to pursue your own interests and inclinations. You had little opportunity to initiate anything on your own. You now feel as if your life was characterized by an extensive string of *have-to*s. You were the puppet on a string, dangling and dancing to the pulls of your director.

We live in a coercive society. We are told to "do this" and "do that" and "don't do this" and "don't do that." The media direct us in the best way to raise our children, brush our teeth, put out the trash, and so on. In business it is common to find the attitude "the only way to get the work done right is to tell them the exact way to do it. Forget this democracy bit! Show them and tell them, and let's forget all the discussion and suggestions. Results count. Let's not waste time."

Most parents sincerely desire the best for their child. They want the child to grow up with his or her own internal sense of right and wrong, and they want the child to be properly self-disciplined. Thus they feel it is important to direct what the child does. They remind him and correct him time and again, until the child feels like a nonentity.

Why do so many parents do this to excess? Where do all their commands come from? They probably come from their own past. Often parents are trying to make up for past deprivations in their own lives. *Should*s and *have to*s become the best way to direct the life of the child.

What do you remember from your past? Were there commands and directives constantly coming your way? Were you encouraged to become your own person and make your own decisions? Were you given an opportunity to develop your own initiative?

Does this method of directing another person's life fulfill its objectives? Does it really work? What does it create along the way? As we said in chapter 2, an overly coerced child may respond in one of three ways:

1. He submits and docilely complies with every demand.
2. He may actively resist for a while, but generally will repress his defiance until he is grown.
3. He resists passively by procrastinating or otherwise showing quiet disagreement with his situation.

However, in some way all of these children resist overcoercion.

Resistance can take several forms when these people grow up. They may resist other people's suggestions and directives. They may resist their own attempts to direct their own lives because they have incorporated their parents' directives and thus have become a parent to themselves. They may see the teachings in Scripture as just another list of *have to*s, thus resisting the Word of God. And they may resist other people.

The Docile Resister

If the overcoercive pattern of control is begun very early in a child's life and is consistent, the child will docilely comply. And this compliance continues throughout his older childhood and adolescence, right into adulthood. He is constantly seeking direction for his life. He finds it difficult to become self-initiated and to make decisions. He responds best to, "You have to do this." He needs other people to prompt him, motivate him, check up on him, and get him moving.

Yet the child who chose to docilely comply to overcoercion can be a resister. How can this be? If you are cooperating, how can you be resisting? A person may learn to docilely follow directions without any kind of resistance. If a parent or older sibling or teacher says "jump," "take out the trash," "come inside," the person responds like an obedient and well-trained dog. He or she doesn't question the commands for fear of losing the love of the commander.

This pattern of responding is easily transferred from parents to other significant people—a Boy Scout leader, teacher, Sunday-school teacher, employer, and so on. Often these significant people reinforce the pattern of compliance by saying, "I just love to have him in my class. There is never a word of back talk. I can always depend upon John. You give him something to do and tell him how to do it, and it gets done. I sure wish the others were like that. Of course, when he's done, he sits and waits for you to tell him the next step. There are times when I wish he would think on his own, but I guess you can't have everything in a person. . . ."

The docile person can actually live a life of terror. He is lost if no one is around telling him what to do or how to do it. He cannot initiate anything on his own, so he spends his time looking for some kind of structure with well-defined tasks and limits.

But how is he resisting overcoercion? This form of resistance is very subtle, but it is directed toward his breaking away from being self-directed. The docile person actually resists himself. He resists the risk of learning how to function and direct his own life. There is safety in being docile. Of course, there are dues to pay, but as long as you have a big brother looking out for you, it seems worth the price.

Are you a docile person? Is this the way you live? Have you considered how this way of life affects you spiritually? You may find yourself gravitating to a church that is dogmatic and dictatorial. You may "buy" what is being taught and preached without ever searching the Scripture yourself. How do you know that what you are being taught is really scripturally true? Do you envision God as another authority figure who simply wants you to comply? Have you considered the fact that He wants you to become less dependent upon others and able to use your own abilities?

God does not want you to be His puppet. He wants you to be a strong, independent person who is able to choose life and make decisions. You may have needed others to direct your life at an early age, but you don't need them now. You are simply holding onto a comfortable life-style. But you need not be locked into it for the rest of your life. There is a different way to live!

The Active Resister

Rather than choosing a docile way of responding, you may have learned at an early age to outwardly resist. No doubt you became aware of some definite attempts by other people to coerce you because they did not like your resistance. Such coercion can take the form of withholding affection and approval.

If you desired affection and approval badly enough, even though you were defiant, you may have learned to comply, but with seething resentment.

As you grow older you are more and more actively resisting other people's attempts to direct your life. This creates some real difficulties. Your automatic reaction when someone gives you a suggestion or directive is to bristle and resist. But being an adult, you realize there are certain consequences when you resist, so you end up accepting the direction. Resentment burns inside you and may flare up in certain comments you make and in sarcasm.

Your childhood perceptions carried over to adulthood may cause you to misperceive suggestions and interpret them as threats. When you become defiant over the supposed threats, you create tension and anxiety. When you do comply, you may live with a perpetual chip on your shoulder.

The Passive Resister

The most common resistive pattern, however, is the passive aggressive. This type of resistance can be very successful for the resister as well as frustrating for the person against whom it is directed. Children accomplish passive aggression with finesse. A child soon learns that an excellent way to create frustration and anger in another person is in passive resistance. It becomes a way of control! But this pattern is actually a form of self-paralysis. An individual caught up in this life-style seldom accomplishes his own goals. He does not live up to his capabilities.

Passive resistance takes many forms. *The most common is procrastination.* A child will dawdle and delay. The phrase a parent hears most is, "Just a minute." The second time the parent calls, the child replies, "Yes, I'm coming," but there is no action. If the child procrastinates long enough, his parent erupts in anger, disapproval, and retribution.

Another characteristic of passive-aggressive behavior is for-

getfulness. Some children (and adults) simply forget what they do not want to remember. (Actually, most forgetting is intentional, whether it is conscious or unconscious.)

Some people use the silent treatment to resist or to push other people away. The person using this device feels powerful and in control. If a spouse or parent chooses to pursue a conversation, he or she is at a loss, because the silent person usually wins.

Another way to resist is by not listening. Some people actually show through their expressions that they are not listening. The less blatant person, however, gives the appearance of being tuned in to his spouse or parent, but in reality, he has clicked off a little switch in his mind and nothing is registering. Some people are so adept at this that periodically they give some type of verbal response to fool the other person: "Uh, huh." "Yes, of course, dear." The body is there, but the mind isn't. This tool is a very effective resistant device.

Being vague in communication is another way to resist. By being noncommittal and vague the passive resister is able to keep his own thoughts, intentions, and feelings to himself. The result is that he pushes others away.

The Result of Resisting

Overcoerced resisters have never learned to be inner directed. When the time comes that they have to be on their own, who guides them? Well, they do. They respond to their own commands, *have to*s, and *should*s with passive resistance. It worked well against other people, and unfortunately, it works well against themselves. Dawdling, daydreaming, and procrastinating are part of their lives. The more pressure they exert upon themselves, the more resistance comes into play. They are full of excuses until some definite pressure from outside of them occurs, and then they resentfully comply.

A writer I know exemplifies this syndrome perfectly. When he was able to produce, his writings sold. But the completed creations have been so few and far between that he and his family barely have enough to eat. Each morning he goes into his room to create. His intentions are admirable. He gives himself a pep talk that he must produce today and sets a goal of half an article by 5:00 P.M. He arranges his resources, sharpens his pencil, checks the typewriter ribbon, makes sure he has paper, and then says, "Now, I'm ready."

But then he feels that he needs a cup of coffee. With coffee cup in hand, he begins to wonder if he has enough ideas for this article. Perhaps it would be better to work on some ideas for some other articles. He searches through some magazines for ideas, then puts the magazines aside and looks out the window for a while, daydreaming. By afternoon he has accomplished very little. He may follow the same pattern for three or four days.

Finally one evening he is frustrated and irritable with his family. He makes several resolutions that evening and determines that tomorrow will be different. He will tackle the original article idea and even complete the entire piece. Fear and anxiety are propelling him because his finances are quite low again. His wife encourages him, but he interprets her statements as pressure.

Passive resistance can crop up in many areas of your life, and your Christian life will reflect it in that your commitments to have a consistent devotional life will be sabotaged. Conviction that some of the things you are doing are contrary to the Christian life will lead you to promise to follow the teachings of the Word of God. But as in other facets of your life, you will resist this promise as well as the teachings. You see God and His Word just as you do everyone else.

Marriages suffer, too. Suppose an overcoerced man marries a woman who is definitely not a coercive person; in fact, she is very nondemanding. However, as we all do, his wife carries certain expectations into their marriage, the normal everyday commonsense tasks of daily living. The husband resists these tasks through procrastination, forgetting, and neglect. What happens in time? The nondemanding wife who at first exerted no pressure is pushed into a coercive role by her partner's lack of involvement.

Now the passive resister husband has a real person to resist. His attitude has created another parent. This ordinarily calm wife has become very irate and verbal because of her husband's continually sloppy and noncompliant behavior. He detests her response to him, and a real cold war begins.

Another way a passive resister resists a spouse is by staying away from home or becoming increasingly involved at work. In fact, excessive absences from home are not only a form of resistance but also serve as punishment and retaliation.

The discovery that one is a resistant person comes as a shock for some people. They have not considered the fact that their behavior follows this pattern. Not everyone who exemplifies these characteristics had overcoercive parents; the pattern could have developed later in life, through interactions with others. But the person who views life as being one big, coercive giant probably is suffering from overcoercion in childhood. There are people today who even resist normal, everyday customs and functions! If they are expected to be on time to work, to eat at a certain time, to cook, to marry, to be polite, to assume responsibility, they continually resist, and serious problems can result.

Can a Resistant Person Change?

Is there any way to escape from this prison of resistance? Yes, but it takes work, for the overcoerced person must develop a new attitude and response to life.

The first step is to identify the directives or commands you are resisting. What are they? Who is really giving them? Are these commands actually coming from your spouse, your friends, your employer, or are you projecting your own reactions against commands onto them?

Where did you get the idea that by following another person's commands or suggestions your life is being controlled?

Have you ever considered the fact that you are still in control when you choose to comply? You probably felt that the only way to be in charge of your life was to resist. Surprise! It isn't! Saying yes to a suggestion or command still leaves you in control. *You* are deciding *Yes, I choose to follow that guideline or suggestion. I have not given myself over to anyone else's control. I am still in charge.* I realize that this way of thinking may be foreign to you. But think about it.

Something else to consider is what your resistance has been accomplishing for you. Is it really helping you achieve what you want in life? Is it worth the lack of productivity and all of the hassles and struggles? Could there be a better way to live? No doubt this pattern has become very comfortable to you. It is automatic and will take effort to break out of it. But you will feel much better about yourself if you work toward change.

Another thing to consider: You want to be in charge of your life, but how do you feel, as an adult, about allowing yourself to be directed and controlled by a rebellious, resistant child inside you? This child is still reacting to your parents' or others' directives toward you; you still hear their voices and commands whenever you attempt to motivate yourself. And you resist yourself. You are not in charge.

Why not use your override ability and say, "Yes, I want to resist this command, but it is something that needs to be done. I can choose to do it, and I know I will feel better by doing it. Right now I am going to stop and pray and ask God to help me give up my resistive pattern and take a positive step of following through. It is possible to do this and move toward being a more mature person."

Part of your resistance may be toward what we call *have to*s. Why not substitute these *have to*s for *want to*s? Many of the things you are resisting are probably those you basically would want to do or feel the necessity of doing, had it not been for someone else telling you that you had to do it. Can you allow the *have to*s to become *want to*s?

A good way to accomplish this will be to complete the following chart. That is, if you *want to* do it. List as many *have to*s from the past and present that you can remember on the left-hand side of the column. Indicate with an asterisk the ones that are currently a problem. In the right-hand column answer the question "Why am I resisting this?"

I have to . . .	Why am I resisting this?

Figure 4

Now take this same list of *have to*s and write them in the form of *want to*s. On the right-hand side of the column, write out what each of these will accomplish in your life.

I want to . . .	This will accomplish . . .

Figure 5

Another way to break out of your pattern of resistive living is to move toward *positive assertive* living. Positive assertive living is neither passive nor aggressive living, nor is it motivated from anger or fear. It is motivated by concern for yourself and for others. Assertive living is not used for the purpose of getting what you want, but to help you live in a free, self-controlled manner. You do not push anyone around, neither yourself nor others.

Positive assertive living begins in your mind—your thoughts and your self-talk. Whenever you say to yourself "I have to" or "others expect this of me," you probably begin to resist. In fact you may think, *They want me to,* or *They expect me to,* whereas in reality they don't. You may have developed ultrasensitive antennae that are picking up some interference and distortion. In some cases, other people may indeed want you to respond in a certain manner. But when you let your self-talk go into action, you begin to feel controlled or pressured; then your automatic pattern of resistance begins to function. Positive, assertive living begins by ridding your mind of distortion and resistant thoughts.

On a piece of paper describe each of the individuals in your life whom you have resisted and are now resisting. What is it that each person did or does that you attempt to resist? Describe exactly how you resist the person, what this accomplishes, and how you feel about the results. What do you expect the other person to do when you resist?

What do you fear would happen if you negotiated a change in the person's request? What would happen if you responded favorably to the request? Have you ever asked these people that you resist if they understand what, why, and how you are resisting? I wonder what would happen if they gave you a request and at the same time also said, "If you want to ignore or resist this request, that's all right." How would you feel? If you have another person who is as concerned about your resistance as you are, ask him to give you both requests and permission to resist. You may be surprised at your response.

Now identify *one* person you are resisting in a way you

know irritates and frustrates him. Indicate what it is you are resisting and then write out three statements that you would be willing to share verbally with this person. Your statement should indicate not only what you do not care to do, but also what you *are* willing to do. Offer positive alternatives in a pleasant manner, and you may find an agreeable response. After all, you don't have that much to lose, do you?

Perhaps the people you think are trying to control you are really trying only to encourage you and exhort you to grow. What might happen if you considered their suggestions in that light? We all need suggestions, help, encouragement, assistance, and guidance from time to time. Consider these statements from Scripture as positive suggestions, not limiting confinements: "He whose ear listens to the life-giving reproof Will dwell among the wise" (Proverbs 15:31 NAS). "He who neglects discipline despises himself, But he who listens to reproof acquires understanding" (Proverbs 15:32 NAS). "Oil and perfume make the heart glad, So a man's counsel is sweet to his friend" (Proverbs 27:9 NAS).

Throughout the book of Proverbs, verse after verse talks about the source of wisdom and guidance for life, how to handle advice and criticism, and the qualities of friendship and relationships with others. Read this book. Consider it. Apply it. It's there to help you resist the pattern you are trapped in. You do not have to let the influence of overcoercive parents or other significant persons in your past continue to rob you of the peace the Lord Jesus promised you.

9

Overcoming Overindulgence

"I've been a Christian for some time now, but I'm still bored and restless. I don't seem to have the peace and contentment other Christians talk about. I'll start something, but the interest just isn't there. Life lacks something for me, but I can't put my finger on it. I feel like a spectator going through life, watching the participants. At times I feel paralyzed and unable to get involved. But at the same time I'm restless! What's wrong with me?"

A cry for help like this is heard over and over again in the counseling office. There are many bored, restless people in our world. Who are they? Why do they feel this way? The person who shared these feelings was probably an overindulged child.[1] When he was a child his parents anticipated what they thought he wanted and needed and gave it to him. They did not wait for him to ask but, instead, provided him with everything he wanted before he made any request. Parents often feel that the best way to express their love for their child is through "showers of blessings." The result is that the child, instead of making known his needs, becomes very passive, waiting for things to be provided. But he also becomes bored and uninterested, because so much is provided for him. His parents, expecting him to be satisfied, soon begin to feel threatened because of his lack of interest; so they give even more to the child to satisfy him, and the cycle is repeated.

Overindulgence is very detrimental because the child is denied the opportunity to learn to experience satisfaction from his own efforts. His growth is stunted because he is kept in a dependent and passive state. He develops the attitude that life is just one big Santa Claus ready to provide him with what he needs. He soon writes off anyone who does not respond in this manner and cater to him. He becomes frustrated because he does not know how to entertain or provide for himself.

An overindulged person does not experience real enjoyment. Rather, he or she tends to concentrate on bad or unsatisfactory experiences. Even though 80 percent of an experience could have been enjoyable, this person focuses upon the remaining 20 percent of unfulfillment. Thus he is insatiable. This passive-dependent child develops into an adult expecting others to cater to him. He subconsciously sets up a pattern of incessant demanding that leads to dissatisfaction, greed, and self-centeredness. Even the attainment of success does not satisfy.

One indication of maturity is the ability to nourish yourself and to experience satisfaction from others nourishing you. But the overindulged person is not able to gratify himself. Some appear so helpless (and they play on this) that you wonder if they might not starve if left to their own devices.

Fear of abandonment is paramount in the overindulged person's mind. Some are phobic about being lonely. And because their dependency tends to drain nourishment from others, after a while they drive other people away. It's difficult to continue your desire to help someone who is never satisfied! Dependency keeps the person from developing his or her own potential. In fact, the person's conscious or unconscious thought probably is: *Why do it myself, if I can get someone else to do it?* Sharing with others is not a consideration! This person has an unusual ability to poison relationships and to put the blame on the other individual. His emotional isolation is a result of his behavior, but he will not accept that fact.

If the overindulged person is forced to fend for himself, he becomes a bit anxious and apprehensive. Then when he does receive some attention, his interest soon wanes, for the only way he can continue to be satisfied is to receive more and more attention.

Overindulged Christians tend to superimpose their life pattern upon Christianity. They expect God to be a continual giver of benefits and blessings. They may look for a church that stresses what God delights in giving to His children; all we have to do is sit back and wait expectantly. They do not care to hear teaching that emphasizes the believer's role in living out the Christian life. Emphasis upon works and giving to others is not their favorite topic.

Why Do Parents Overindulge Their Children?

Are you a parent who tends to overindulge your child? Or were you an overindulged child? Why does a parent do this? There are several reasons.

Overindulging another person may be the parent's way of *fulfilling his own needs.* Some adults have excessive needs to give affection or to "mother" others, which can also include attempting to protect the child from the normal adjustments of life that are necessary for development. Jane, a middle-aged mother, came into the office with her two children. They seemed well-behaved but appeared unhappy. After observing Jane's interaction with them, I soon learned why! She told them where to sit, when and how to blow their noses, and when they were thirsty. When I asked them questions, she helped them answer. She also talked about her delight in being able to be such a "good and competent" mother to them.

Overindulgence may be *a way of life* for some people. Some parents are so wealthy that it is no problem to give and give and give. They overindulge themselves, their family members, and even other people as a way of life and also as a way of competing with other wealthy friends.

George never spent any time with his only son. He was too busy at his business. But George, Jr., never lacked for anything. He didn't have one bicycle—he had three, and all were the most expensive models. George bragged to his friends about how well he treated his son. At times George was a bit perplexed about why George, Jr., wasn't as grateful as he hoped he'd be.

Some parents may overindulge their children *out of guilt.* The guilt-ridden parent is a prime target for either abusing a child or catering to him. The guilt may very well be the result of abusing the child or it may stem from his own past or an unsatisfactory marital relationship. This kind of person can relieve some of his guilt by overindulging a child.

Denise was so angry when she walked into the office. "That child runs me ragged. She wants this, and she wants that. I can never give her enough."

I asked her, "What happens when you tell her no?"

"I try, but I can't. The guilt overwhelms me. I want her to be happy and have what I didn't, but it's not working." Guilt motivation digs the pit deeper and deeper.

A larger group of overindulging parents, however, are those who have come from a *background of deprivation.* Time and time again I have heard parents say, "My child will not have to crawl up through life the way I did. I'll make it easier for him." But the parent is actually living his own life through the child. He is making up for his own childhood deprivation by vicariously living through his child. Some parents are blind to the effects this has upon the child. Others continue to respond to their child's boredom and listlessness by giving them even more. Some parents even get angry at their child's lack of response and see the child as unappreciative. But in time the pattern of giving continues.

Results of Overindulgence

How does overindulgence manifest itself in a person's life? Let's look at some of the common characteristics:

Mind reading is a common problem between married couples whom I see in counseling. As one wife put it: "Why should I have to tell him what my needs are? We have been married for eleven years, and you would think he would know by now. He should be able to sense what I want! Telling another person what you need takes the excitement and romance out of a relationship. He can figure it out."

Statements like that are common—and frustrating! The overindulged person has a greater need to have others read his or her mind than does the rest of humanity. After all, their parents read their minds. They did not have to ask for much because their parents responded to their every whim. Why not now? "Read my mind, anticipate, and provide" is their life motto in friendships, at work, and in their marriage.

Expecting someone to read your mind puts tremendous pressure upon the other person for several reasons. For one, it is impossible to read another person's mind, no matter how long you have known that person. How can you cooperate if it is impossible? And even if you try, it is pure guesswork. Your intentions may be noble, but the results can still be disastrous. You may try to figure out what your spouse wants for dinner and go all out, fixing a fantastic gourmet meal. How devastating when the response is: "Well, you should have known that I wanted roast tonight and not this stuff."

Life for the overindulged is full of *shoulds* and *oughts* directed toward other people: "You ought to know that I wanted this." And when you fail to read his mind, he feels that you do not love him, because you are not meeting his needs as his parents did.

Another characteristic of the overindulged person is his *inability to make other people feel good.* In fact, he often attempts to make them feel indebted to him. If they do not respond in this way, the overindulged individual has numerous ways of making them feel selfish or worthless. An overindulged parent may thank his grown son or daughter for visiting him and in the same breath add that the child doesn't come as often as he should.

In a marriage relationship, the overindulged person *does not listen.* The spouse will attempt to make his or her point, but for some reason it does not penetrate. In fact, some married couples repeat the same argument for years, with no resolution.

If your spouse is *constantly dissatisfied,* you may be living with an overindulged person, for such people do not stay happy very long. Sometimes they even whine when their needs are not met. You may find yourself constantly being blamed for your spouse's unhappiness. And if you do not indulge him, you may find your spouse turning against you, which can come as a shock. Your spouse may even seek satisfaction elsewhere, and you will be blamed.

In his own way the overindulged person is very demanding, but he often does it passively. He lives with hundreds of hidden expectations, and if other people cannot read his mind, they are insensitive and unloving.

What a setup! What a way to cripple a relationship. You have demands placed upon you, but you aren't even aware of what they are. There are serious negative consequences when such demands are placed upon a marital partner. Dr. Joseph Maxwell describes these consequences.

> Most of us are not aware of the demands we make on our spouse to exhibit certain traits or behaviors. What we are aware of is the feeling of anger or annoyance we experience when we are frustrated in realizing our demands. The feeling is so strong, so dependable, so apparently autonomous that we think it is not only justified, but unavoidable. We believe that the feeling is caused by our spouse's failure rather than our demand. This occurs because we are very aware of the failure but are largely unaware of the demand which designates the failure as a bad event.
>
> Demandingness is a formidable barrier to marital growth because the person doing the demanding is likely to spend most of his or her time and energy catastrophizing and pitying self, and to spend little creative energy in

planning ways to develop the relationship. Since every behavior of a spouse necessarily evokes a responsive behavior from the other spouse, such personally upsetting
behavior as is produced by demandingness will usually
have significant effects on the actions and feelings of the
partner. In most cases, when one partner reacts negatively
the other one responds by behaving equally negatively,
creating an endless cycle of demandingness that leads
away from growth and development of the relationship.

If only one spouse is willing to give up his or her demandingness, the cycle can not only be stopped, but re-
versed toward strengthening the marriage.[2]

There is no way any person can "just know" what the other
person desires. The belief that a person deserves to have what
he wants with or without asking is an archaic feeling from the
past that will keep his life stunted and lifeless. The infantile
fantasies that have never been resolved present major obstacles
to the development of a healthy and positive relationship. If,
however, you desire a parent-child marriage and you fill your
own needs by overindulging your spouse, then you may be satisfied. But the relationship does not provide a healthy, balanced marriage.

In time the spouse who has so many subtle and unspoken
demands placed upon him may feel like checking out of the
marital relationship. He gets tired of always being on the giving end, never on the receiving.

Forms of Indulgence

It is important to realize that at one time or another we all
indulge ourselves, and this indulgence may have nothing
to do with our childhood. We may want to treat ourselves
better than we were treated as a child because we can clearly
point to a time in our childhood when we experienced a lack.
Or we may have developed in adult life a strong liking
for some hobby or interest and, in a sense, it has become

our "weakness." It gives us real satisfaction to pursue this interest.

The truly overindulged person, on the other hand, feels deprived but cannot pinpoint a time in his past when he lacked anything. None of his pursuits are satisfying to him. He still feels that others owe it to him to provide for him without any effort or work on his part. We often refer to such people as "spoiled" or "selfish"—strong words, but they are accurate.

Dr. Hugh Missildine describes several of the more common forms that overindulgence can take.[3]

Alcohol can be a form of self-indulgence. When a person feels bored and lonely, it is easy to use the effects of the alcohol to overcome those unpleasant feelings. But this dependency soon leads to other personal and interpersonal difficulties.

The *handling of money* can be a source of continual trauma. A child grows up not knowing how to handle money and perhaps lacks a knowledge of the value of it. He buys and is momentarily happy, but his happiness soon fades and he is bored again. So the answer is to buy more. If the cash is not available, why not use the plastic money, which is available? But dissatisfaction is always present. Since he may not have learned to apply himself in either education or his job, funds may be limited, and he becomes bitter toward a society that does not respond to his every whim.

Clothes seem to be a favorite form of overindulgence, more so with women than with men. The indulgence is not limited to articles of clothing, but to accessories, jewelry, and other items. Rationalization is easy: "Who wants to be out of fashion?" And continual purchases are made. But the delight and enjoyment of these newly purchased items are soon lost.

What about *food?* The causes of overeating are too numerous to list, but overindulgence is definitely one of them. Some children may not have been overindulged in anything except food. They developed preferences for certain foods and strong dislike for others. These preferences easily carry over into adulthood. Food becomes an excellent way to help us feel better when we are down.

Marriage receives a great deal of the fallout from the pattern of overindulgence. An overindulged husband, for example, who is *unable to take initiative,* has difficulty developing a deep, intimate relationship with his wife. Most of his relationships are shallow, including his relationship with his wife. He always allows someone else to carry the load. The cause of his unhappiness is always "out there," for he lacks the insight to realize that the source of it is actually within. Blame and more blame. He and his wife begin to drift apart, which is probably what happened in his relationships prior to marriage. Single life was a disappointment, and now so is marriage. Some will marry and then divorce, looking for their happiness, seeking an elusive provider who in reality is a phantom developed by their incessant needs. When that doesn't work out or when they find someone who has a "giving well" of immense depth, they may choose to marry yet again. But either way, boredom and the "entertain me" attitude persist.

Passive overindulged adults soon learn that in order to survive they will need to learn ways of responding and behaving that will bring them what they desire. They become very adept at appearing needy in a way that encourages others to give to them. Some become clever at drawing sympathy for the things they lack. But unlike a true con artist, they cannot carry this off to a conclusion. Con artists work others in a clever manner to get what they want, usually purporting to represent some worthy cause. The overindulged, however, shows little interest or concern for those about him. Even those he sincerely likes may tire of constantly being expected to give to him. For the more they give to him, the more passive he becomes. In time he actually pushes away those who are giving him what he wants!

Are You a Victim of the Overindulged Child?

How can you tell if an overindulged child of the past is still running your life? It undoubtedly is if you subscribe to the following belief: "Other people should take the initiative and cater to me without my having to participate in any way, including telling them what I need and want. I have no responsibility to meet their needs or show interest in them as persons or reciprocate in any way."

If you are bothered because other people want you to "take responsibility," overindulgence is your pattern! But is your overindulgent attitude working? Is it bringing you happiness and satisfaction?

You are actually using your own weakness to control other people. You are sending the message: "I need to be taken care of by you, and I expect it." By being helpless and dependent you are tying other people to you with a leash. But the dependent person soon becomes a drag on a relationship. There is an old-fashioned word for this pattern—*self-centered*. And there is another term that applies also—*narcissism*.

The narcissistic person is concerned only for his own needs and feels he is so special that life should revolve around him. He feels entitled to whatever makes him happy and expects special favors without assuming reciprocal responsibilities. If other people do not respond, he is surprised and angry. He takes advantage of others to indulge his own desires or to make himself look good. He disregards the rights and integrity of others, and he has no empathy at all. He is unable to recognize how others feel, and he does not appreciate it when they are upset or distressed. His self-esteem is fragile, even though it appears to be very strong indeed.

We might sum up the needs and demands of the overindulged person as follows. The other person in the relationship must:

> ... be exactly what the overindulged person wants him to be at any given time.
> ... make no demands upon him and be satisfied with living in the vacuum the overindulged person creates.
> ... anticipate his wishes, wants, and desires by reading his mind or "just knowing" what he wants.

... not change or grow in ways that would cause the person to no longer be able to meet his needs.

If there is a problem in the relationship, it is the other person's fault, because he does not love the overindulged person sufficiently. If the other person does not meet all his needs, it may be all right to look elsewhere for someone who will.

You Can Change

If you are a victim of this child of your past and would like to move from dependency to independence, it can be done. It will not be easy because it takes both a sincere desire to change and the uncomfortable experience of forcing yourself to act contrary to your tendencies. However, if you are dissatisfied with your life, there is a better way to live. You can be a more independent person! You do not have to continue to be self-centered and narcissistic.

Take a piece of paper and pencil and describe in detail the relationship you now have with your spouse or another person who is close to you. Be as specific as you can describing how you talk and act around this person and how you use or rely upon him or her. Now describe in detail a totally different relationship with this person. Visualize yourself as a strong, balanced person who can both give and receive. As you write, see yourself as content and satisfied with this new relationship.

Now think with me about a new life-style. Go into a room and shut yourself away from anything that might distract you. Be sure the phone is off the hook and conditions are such that you won't be disturbed. Sit in a comfortable chair and take some deep breaths and let all of the air out in one large release. Accept the belief that you can no longer live the type of life you have been experiencing.

Create a visual image in your mind of a life in which you are able to give as well as receive, in which you are satisfied and content. See yourself following through with the same tasks, relationships, and involvements you already have in your life, but this time you are not a drain upon others. Rather, you are nourishing them.

After creating this image see yourself in a room with a pleasant atmosphere. You are comfortable and relaxed. There is a knock at the door, and you arise to answer the knock. Upon opening the door you are surprised and delighted to find Jesus standing there. You invite Him in, and He enters. He looks at you and smiles and then says, "I came to share something with you, My friend. You are a capable, self-reliant person. I want you to know that and believe that. If you have taken Me into your life then you have greater potential and strength than you realize. You can give to others. You no longer have to be a taker. I want you to give your life out of My abundance, which I have given to you, and I want you to discover all of your hidden capabilities you have never realized. Do this, and you will discover a new life. I care for you, and I love you. I am for you, and I desire that you be for yourself as well."

Jesus turns and smiles at you as He leaves. He has affirmed you. Now you can *live as an affirmed person.*

When you have completed this experience, take the time to write out your feelings. Take your time so that feelings and thoughts can surface. When you finish, describe in writing the type of person and life you now want to live. Pray for a vision of service to others.

Here are several practical suggestions to follow so you will have both structure and a definite plan to follow.

1. If you find yourself retreating into the same old pattern of thinking and living, repeat your visualization experience, including the writing exercise. Read and meditate on the following verses: "But let all things be done properly and in an orderly manner" (1 Corinthians 14:40 NAS). "I can do all things through Him who strengthens me" (Philippians 4:13 NAS). "And let endurance have its perfect result, that you may be perfect and complete, lacking in

nothing" (James 1:4 NAS). "A new commandment I give to you, that you love one another, even as I have loved you, that you also love one another" (John 13:34 NAS). "Bear one another's burdens, and thus fulfill the law of Christ" (Galatians 6:2 NAS). "For you were called to freedom, brethren; only do not turn your freedom into an opportunity for the flesh, but through love serve one another" (Galatians 5:13 NAS). "Do nothing from selfishness or empty conceit, but with humility of mind let each of you regard one another as more important than himself" (Philippians 2:3 NAS).

2. Make a complete list of the areas of your life that you would like to see improved, in relationship to others. Continue writing until the list is complete.

3. Make another list of the three individuals you are closest to. What are their concerns and needs? If you are not aware of their needs, ask them what their needs are and how you could minister to them in a better way. Keep track of your daily ministerings to others. Place no demands or requests at all.

Inwardly, as you are doing these exercises, you may be crying out and feeling helpless and anxious. But in time these feelings will lessen and you will discover a quiet and solid satisfaction as you enter a new life-style. You may find other people voluntarily beginning to minister to you in a new way! Wouldn't that be exciting? Imagine another person taking the initiative to love and accept you without your having to hint, manipulate, suggest, whine, complain, or pressure them! What a difference when people begin to respond to you out of their own sincere desire.

It may take days, weeks, or months, and being patient may be difficult. But it will pay off in time. Set no expectations for the behavior of others. Their respone to you is not why you are taking these steps. It is for *your* benefit and development as a true child of God. When you feel the urge to request something from someone, replace it with the thought (and in some cases the action, as well), *How can I meet that person's needs?*

If you find yourself straying back into your old pattern, ask yourself the following questions:

1.   Is this what I really want and what is best for me?
2.   What will this accomplish?
3.   Why am I allowing myself to revert back to this old pattern?
4.   What can I now do to return to my new way of living?
5.   What can I do the next time to keep me from reverting?

Be sure to write down your responses to these questions. Your tendency may be to avoid the writing because you feel it puts more pressure upon you to change. It does! And that's good!

Remember this: Your needs have been met and filled already. You may not yet feel that they have, but because of who Jesus Christ is and what He has done for you, you have been made sufficient. Your task is to appropriate what He has already given you.

How Are Your Needs Fulfilled?

How do you get love from others? By reaching out to them, even if it means acting contrary to the way you feel. Instead of being a taker, you become a giver. How? By accepting God's declaration of who you are and what you are. As John Powell puts it:

> There is one need so fundamental and so essential that if it is met, everything else will almost certainly harmonize in a general sense of well-being. When this need is properly nourished, the whole human organism will be healthy and the person will be happy. This need is a true and deep appreciation of oneself, a genuine and joyful self-

acceptance, an authentic self esteem, which results in an interior sense of celebration. It is good to be me ... I am very happy to be me.[4]

"But," you say, "isn't this my problem? Don't I have an inflated sense of who I am?" Do you really? Or have you been fooling yourself all these years? Isn't your dependency a cover up because deep down you question who you are and your ability? We can only give to others when we have a balanced acceptance of ourselves. This self-acceptance is a gift from God. His love to us is an unconditional commitment to imperfect persons. When your feelings of inadequacy and helplessness are disposed of and you discover you can take care of yourself, your need to be taken care of will go away. To accomplish this you must begin to minister to others.

There are five basic needs of life as developed by Abraham Maslow. First, our *physical needs* must be met, the need for air, water, food—whatever is necessary to keep us alive. Second, we have the need for *safety,* security, and freedom from danger. For most of us these two basic needs are not a problem, for they are met on a daily basis.

But the next three are where we often get hung up: the need for *love and belonging* (being wanted, cared about, listened to, accepted, understood, and made to feel important); the need for *self-esteem* (receiving attention, respect, significance, value, achieving goals); and the need for *self-actualization* (the ability to give love—*agape*—and to fulfill one's potential or giftedness).

Lawrence Crabb writes:

> A sign of maturity is the ability to give to others and to meet others' needs. But it appears that in order to do this, we must have the first four levels of needs met. As Christians, you and I have a greater opportunity to have our needs met than others. God has promised to meet all of the needs indicated on Maslow's list. God has met our physical needs. "Seek ye first the kingdom of God, and his righteousness; and all these things (referring to food,

clothing, shelter) shall be added unto you" (Matt. 6:33). God has met our need to know that tomorrow our physical needs will be met. "Take therefore no (anxious) thought for tomorrow" (Matt. 6:34). "Be anxious for nothing, but in everything ... let your requests be made known to God ... my God shall supply all your needs according to His riches in glory in Christ Jesus" (Phil. 4:6, 19). God has met our need for security (love). "Who shall separate us from the love of God, which is in Christ Jesus" (Rom. 8:35, 38, 39). "God commendeth his love toward us, in that, while we were yet sinners (at our worst, exposed for what we really are, no masks), Christ died for us" (Rom. 5:8). God has met our need for significance (purpose). "For to me to live is Christ and to die is gain" (Phil. 1:21). "For we are his workmanship, created in Christ Jesus unto good works, which God hath before ordained that we should walk in them" (Eph. 2:10). "(God) redeemeth thy life from destruction (squandering, wasting)" (Ps. 103:4).

To the degree that a Christian believes these verses, he is freed from a life of self-centered concern with whether or not his own needs are met, and he is able to move on to real self-actualization, confidently knowing (not necessarily always "feeling") that his physical needs will be met according to God's purposes and that his personal needs are now and forever perfectly met. To believe this in the face of tremendous pressure to agree with the world's false value system of living for money, pleasure, or fame requires a strong commitment to the authority of Scripture.

Christians never operate from a deficit but rather from fullness. Our lives should be an expression of that fullness in worship and service. I therefore refer to the motivation of an appropriately self-actualized person as Expression Motivation. Yet most of us feel a deficit and act in ways designed to fill the void. It is one thing to say that we can claim by faith that our needs are already met in God and therefore live in Stage 5 with Expression Motivation. It is quite another thing to disentangle ourselves successfully from the sticky web of deficit motivation.[5]

You and I need not operate from a deficit. We are filled people! We can have the love, attention, and acceptance we want. But often we go after it in reverse. Become a participant instead of a spectator. You are loved. Respond to others out of that love. You can break free of the overindulged child within you. But it's your choice.

Healing Emotional Paralysis

I work with many people who are paralyzed and immobilized by fear: fear of making a decision, fear of disapproval, fear of taking a stand, fear that other people do not like them, and—the worst fear—fear of breaking out of this pattern of life they are trapped in.

Physical paralysis is a terrible thing. To be locked up, immobilized so that your body cannot function and cannot respond to the messages of your mind, is very frustrating. But it is even more frustrating when the paralysis is a limitation not of the body but of the mind. We have been talking about areas of weakness in our minds that keep us bound to our past and prevent us from becoming mature. All these things can cause us to come under the control of fear. And fear paralyzes us so that we cannot make the necessary changes that will lead to growth.

The Bible tells us about a man who was paralyzed in his mind (emotionally) as well as in his body:

> After these things there was a feast of the Jews; and Jesus went up to Jerusalem. Now there is in Jerusalem by the sheep gate a pool, which is called in Hebrew Bethesda, having five porticos. In these lay a multitude of those who

were sick, blind, lame, withered. And a certain man was there, who had been thirty-eight years in his sickness. When Jesus saw him lying there, and knew that he had already been a long time in that condition, He said to him, "Do you wish to get well?" The sick man answered Him, "Sir, I have no man to put me into the pool when the water is stirred up, but while I am coming, another steps down before me." Jesus said to him, "Arise, take up your pallet, and walk." And immediately the man became well, and took up his pallet and began to walk.

John 5:1–9 NAS

The man in this account had been paralyzed for thirty-eight years. He lay by this pool day after day, waiting for a way to be free of his affliction. Beneath this famous pool, which was actually deep enough for people to swim in, was a subterranean stream. Every now and then the stream bubbled up and disturbed the waters of the pool. The Jewish people believed that this disturbance was caused by an angel, and the first person to get into the pool while it was bubbling would be healed from any illness.

When Jesus discovered the lame man by the pool, He asked him one of the strangest questions in all of Scripture: "Do you want to be healed?" Or to put it another way, "Do you want to change?" I suppose the man was rather taken aback by Jesus' seemingly unsympathetic question. Didn't Jesus understand that he had been brought to this pool day after day, week after week, year after year, for healing? Didn't Jesus understand that he had asked person after person to help him get into the pool?

Or could it be that Jesus knew what was really going on inside this man, and that is why He asked the question. It is possible that after so many years of frustration in the same state of paralysis the man's helplessness had turned into hopelessness. Perhaps all hope for healing had died, and in its place was a dull despair. His answer seems to indicate this, for instead of just replying, "Yes," he gave as an answer the reason why he could not be healed. He would go through the motions each day of trying to get into the pool, but in his heart perhaps he believed that he would never touch the water.

Or is it possible that he had actually achieved a degree of contentment in being an invalid for the rest of his life? If he were cured, he would have to assume some new responsibilities, such as finding a job. Other people would expect much more of him than they did now.

Whatever the man's inner condition, Jesus tells him exactly what to do. He actually told the man to do the impossible—to get up and walk and to carry his bed with him. When Jesus said this, the man trusted Him, and he got up! The atrophy in his legs disappeared, and he immediately began to walk.

Consider Jesus' question for your own life, "Do you want to be healed? Do you want to change?" Each of us must ponder this question fully before responding. There is a cost involved in changing. Making any change means giving up something that is very familiar, even though it is detrimental to you. You will have to experience growth pains and emotional discomfort. The reactions and responses of other people toward you will change, and some of their reactions may be very uncomfortable. You can no longer predict how people will treat you. New responsibilities may become a part of your life. Attention or sympathy you received in the past will no longer be available. Higher expectations may be had of you.

The man at the pool discovered almost immediately that this change in his life was going to cost him. He got in trouble with the religious leaders before he even had time to rejoice over his physical and emotional healing. The day he was healed happened to be the Sabbath, and the man was caught carrying his bed. The Jews told him, ". . . It is not lawful for thee to carry thy bed" on the Sabbath (John 5:10). This undoubtedly was only the first of many challenges this man had to meet as a result of his new life.

It must be your decision to break out of your paralyzing style of living, no one else can make that decision for you. But when you do, you will begin to feel the freedom of release from the paralyzing effects of fear.

What are some of the ways you can be immobilized by fear?

Giving in to People

One of the most common forms of paralysis is being overly submissive or compliant. This malady is evident by constantly giving in to other people and their requests or demands on you. You defer to them, overriding your own feelings and desires. Because of personal insecurity and self-doubt, you continually comply with the wishes of others. You question your own ability and decisions. You want to avoid conflict and altercations. Your feelings are often characterized by the title of a popular book *When I Say No I Feel Guilty*. But there are no rational reasons for this feeling. Your pattern of behavior simply reflects your own insecurities about your capabilities. It is also reflective of a strong need to please and have the approval of those around you—both friends and strangers.

One of my former clients described very clearly the pattern of his life.

> I was the oldest of five children. And because of this my parents gave me more responsibility. I found that I could please them and gain their approval by being good. Whatever they wanted me to do I would do. I realized that other children were out playing, but not only was I doing what my parents asked, I would ask them for ways to help. I continued this pattern even during college. I became overly conscientious about work. I would more than give my time and even deduct an hour a day from my time card to make sure I had given the company the correct time. And now I have more work and responsibilities than I can ever meet because I cannot say no to any request. I have some personal relationships that I want to be free of but I give in to their requests. I say no to them, write them letters saying no, but because I am such a pushover and they know it, they keep on asking. They know I'll give in. I get so angry inside. But I always smile and comply. I'm so mad at myself I want to do something for myself for a change. But I can't.

Seeking Approval

Another type of emotional paralysis is found in those who constantly seek the approval of others. The search for approval is neverending because the emotionally paralyzed person's need for this is insatiable. It is never enough, never permanent, never satisfying. To gain acceptance, the person takes on the role of a worker or helper. He approaches each task feverishly, working up a cycle of positive reinforcement. If he helps someone and the person responds affirmatively, he feels worthwhile. But because he is not convinced of his own worth, this pattern has to be repeated. He is influenced more by what he thinks will please others than by his own desires. He is a victim of his feelings and needs. This in turn generates a self-hatred because he feels less of a person than he should be. He has such strong inner doubts and fears that the message of approval and acceptance must be repeated again and again. It is a broken record of redundancy that he never really believes. If he did, he could turn it off.

Compliance—being in submission to others—at the proper time and for the appropriate purpose is important. But to submit because of a compelling search for approval is a form of paralysis. Those who do this believe that the way to please themselves is to please others. They have the misbelief that "having the approval of others will give me all of the satisfaction and positive feelings about myself that I need for my life." Dr. William Knaus says that "getting high on the admiration of others results in emotional drunkenness."[1]

We all desire approval to varying degrees. Some seek approval at any cost. Others seem to take it or leave it. But when you feel a strong need for approval, you tend to become a pawn of your own urgency. You begin to be so dominated by the quest that you lose perspective on the other areas of your life. Mental gymnastics become the essence of your life. You carry on an endless debate such as, *Should I say it this way or that way? Should I smile or not? I wonder if I should wait until everyone else is seated before I walk in or go in now? I wonder what he will think if I say this? Boy, I sure don't want to sound stupid. I'm not sure if I should say anything at all now. Or maybe I should!*

Constantly trying to predict what others will think or feel about you is an exercise in futility. These internal debates keep you from expressing an idea or opinion that may be different from others. Thus you end up giving the appearance of being tongue-tied or not having anything to say. Your fear stops you. Once again you are back to your paralysis.

Not everyone responds to this need by saying nothing, however. In order to gain approval, some people become quite wishy-washy by complying with the beliefs of others. They continually give in to others' requests, beliefs, or directives. They sell out even to the enemy, which creates an ongoing conflict. They dislike themselves for not holding to their own opinions, standards, and beliefs. Yet the need for approval overrides their desires to stand on their own two feet.

But does this kind of person ever get the approval he seeks? Do other people really think highly and admirably of him? Or do they think that the approval seeker has no backbone, no opinions, no standards—that "he can be conned into doing whatever I want him to do"? Does the approval seeker generate respect or disrespect? Is he viewed as a doormat or someone with inner strength?

Being the "Good Guy"

Acting weak and passive is one way to gain approval. But there are other ways, such as becoming the "good guy" or "good gal." The "good guy" gives favors to other people and is overly friendly. He feels it is all right if he inwardly resents the other person who he feels is taking advantage of him. Actually the other person is just taking him up on his offer. Because he grants favors to others and says yes so much, the "good guy" may find himself overwhelmed with obligations. He reacts by putting off what he says he will do. No one could possibly accomplish all he commits himself to, and his resentment hinders his desire to comply. He now begins to create the image of a procrastinator. And other people begin to wonder about him. They may even become angry because of his failure to follow through. Now where is the approval he was looking for?

Much of the disapproval we fear is not going to happen! It is simply a worry. We anticipate and fear the worst, so we become both internal and external procrastinators.

Avoiding Social Contacts

The opposite of the "good guy" is the person who avoids all social contacts. We call him shy, but he is actually afraid of people. This tendency is often a form of withdrawal that he learned very early in childhood. In contrast to the person who is constantly seeking approval, the shy person expects to be rejected. Social gatherings are terrible experiences for him.

Shy people suffer under the belief, "people are my enemies. They cannot wait to reject me. They are out there lurking about, just waiting for me to make contact. And why shouldn't they want to reject me? I'm not as smart or as attractive or as articulate as they are. If I reach out, I will blow it as always." Their own negative evaluation of themselves, which they project onto others, inhibits their response.

Dr. William Knaus has suggested that those who are shy live with a number of myths. These myths are falsely based beliefs which are nothing more than rationalizations.

The *First Impression* myth is the belief that unless you make a perfect impression when meeting someone for the first time, disaster will be the result. You are hesitant about meeting people because you are not sure that you are going to make a good impression.

The *Perfectly Articulate Person* myth is the belief that unless you are highly skilled in verbal communication, you had better refrain from sharing anything with another person.

Another frequently used myth is the *Perfect Opening Line*. "If I knew how to open a conversation in the proper manner, then I would." This is a sure way to avoid starting conversations.

The myth of *Perfect Preparation* suggests that you should not speak up in a group of people unless you are highly conversant with the latest political view, magazine, best-selling novel, and so on. If you are not up on everything, you are going to be at a disadvantage.

The importance of *Being Comfortable and Relaxed* in a group before you ever open up is another myth which impedes people from interpersonal contact.

There is also the *Savior* myth, which is the hope that you will be protected and rescued by another person, who will take charge of your life for you.

A myth that is reinforced by ads and television is the belief that in order to succeed socially you have to be the *Life of the Party*. You must be free, open, expressive, happy, fun loving, not too serious, and so on.[2]

Who do you try to please? Are you seeking so desperately for approval and acceptance that you are selling yourself to others for a few words of praise? Do you realize that you are paralyzed?

How to Take up Your Bed and Walk

Would you like to develop the ability to express your own thoughts and feelings openly? Would you like to be able to say no to someone or something and still feel comfortable? Would you like to be able to voice your disagreements and not have butterflies do acrobatics in your stomach? Would you like to be able to share warm, positive feelings without being overly concerned about the response to your offer to care?

There is hope for the internal and external procrastinator. But, first, consider these questions:

Are you satisfied and happy with your present life and circumstances?

If there is the possibility of responding in a different way, would you be willing to consider it?

Are you living your life now out of your own strength and abilities or out of the abundance of inner strength and wisdom that God has made available to you through Jesus Christ and the ministry of the Holy Spirit?

What is the worst thing that could happen if you tried any of the suggestions and they didn't work out to your satisfaction? If you are afraid of disapproval, you are already living a self-rejecting life. You believe that others will reject you, so what would be new if they did? I think you will be surprised. The following suggestions are going to sound frightening, ridiculous, and even foreign to anything you may have thought of doing. But all it will take is one successful experience in ten to have a better experience than you have now. The odds are not that bad. But it's your choice. Why not believe in you as God believes in you?

If you seek approval too much: Do you feel that saying no is all right, especially without giving any reasons? If not, practice saying no a number of times. Go to a store and look at a number of items for sale, but do not buy any. Just keep saying, "No, thank you."

What is wrong with saying no or maybe? Why is saying yes all right, when inwardly you do not mean yes?

Write down at least three positive changes you would like to see in other people's behavior toward you. Put them in a very positive manner, such as something you would appreciate them doing.

Say either, "No," or, "Let me think about that a minute," at least three times this week.

If you are always the first to volunteer or are the first to arrive or the last to leave in order to help, reverse your usual response. Give someone else the opportunity to serve.

If you always try to be witty or tell jokes in order to gain approval or attention, back off. Allow some of the others to carry the fun and conversation.

With a friend practice taking back an item to a store that is noted for not giving cheerful refunds.

Change some of your typical ways of responding. If you are always smiling around the office, appear more serious. Change your style of dress. If you dress to gain attention, tone it down. If you dress to fit in, wear something bold and colorful. If you tend to give your opinion first, ask others their opinion. If you tend not to share your opinion until you see what others believe or feel, share yours first.

If you are struggling with shyness and fear of rejection: Identify which of the myths you own. How often are you conscious of making statements like those to yourself? Keep a list. Write down your challenge to them.

As you practice your visual imagery, take each myth one at a time and practice seeing yourself interacting with others as though you did not believe that myth. Imagine yourself in a successful interaction and feeling good about yourself.

Each day practice saying hello to three people whom you do not know. Ask at least one stranger a day what time it is. Keep doing these exercises until you feel comfortable. Maintain eye contact with others as you speak to them.

If you are fearful of going into a store alone or eating alone in a restaurant, face this fear by going alone. While there, be friendly to the waitress and ask two or three questions that show your interest in her as a person.

Wear a button with a meaning that must be explained for it to make sense. Create one of your own. By doing this you will be surprised at the number of people who will ask you what it means.

These suggestions may seem frightening, but rehearsing them in your mind or verbally with a friend lessens the threat. Why not begin to act as though others will accept you? Most people will!

It is possible to become assertive—socially skilled and able to share yourself with others rather than holding it all inside. Being assertive is more than sharing complaints or being insistent in a proper way. It's the ability to experience your own potential and strength. It involves expressing your own thoughts and feelings openly, including warmth and affection, hopes, fears. It is the calm assurance of being able to say no and not hold thoughts and feelings inside. This builds healthy, positive, and long-lasting relationships.

Are you assertive and to what degree? Use the following questions to determine your level of assertion.

Assertion Questionnaire

Column A, below, indicates your frequency of assertion.

Indicate how often each of these events occurred by marking Column A, using the following scale:

1. This has not happened in the past 30 days.
2. This has happened a few times (1 to 6 times) in the past 30 days.
3. This has happened often (7 times or more) in the past 30 days.

Column B indicates how you feel about assertion.

Indicate how you feel about each of these events by marking Column B, using the following scale:

1. I felt very uncomfortable or upset when this happened.
2. I felt somewhat uncomfortable or upset when this happened.
3. I felt neutral when this happened (neither comfortable nor uncomfortable, neither good nor upset).
4. I felt fairly comfortable or good when this happened.
5. I felt very comfortable or good when this happened.

Important: If an event has not happened during the past month, then rate it according to how you think you would feel if it happened. If an event happened more than once in the past month, rate roughly how you felt about it on the average.

	A	B

1. Turning down a person's request to borrow my car.
2. Asking a favor of someone.
3. Resisting sales pressure.
4. Admitting fear and requesting consideration.
5. Telling a person I am intimately involved with that he/she has said or done something that bothers me.
6. Admitting ignorance in an area being discussed.
7. Turning down a friend's request to borrow money.
8. Turning off a talkative friend.
9. Asking for constructive criticism.
10. Asking for clarification when I am confused about what someone has said.
11. Asking whether I have offended someone.
12. Telling a person of the opposite sex that I like him or her.
13. Telling a person of the same sex that I like him or her.
14. Requesting expected service when it hasn't been offered (such as, in a restaurant).
15. Discussing openly with a person his or her criticism of my behavior.
16. Returning defective items (such as, at a store or restaurant).
17. Expressing an opinion different from that of a person I am talking with.
18. Telling someone how I feel if he or she has done something that is unfair to me.
19. Turning down a social invitation from someone I don't particularly like.
20. Resisting pressure to drink.
21. Resisting an unfair demand from a person who is important to me.

		A	B
22.	Requesting the return of borrowed items.		
23.	Telling a friend or co-worker when he or she says or does something that bothers me.		
24.	Asking a person who is annoying me in a public situation to stop (such as, smoking on a bus).		
25.	Criticizing a friend.		
26.	Criticizing my spouse.		
27.	Asking someone for help or advice.		
28.	Expressing my love to someone.		
29.	Asking to borrow something.		
30.	Giving my opinion when a group is discussing an important matter.		
31.	Taking a definite stand on a controversial issue.		
32.	When two friends are arguing, supporting the one I agree with.		
33.	Expressing my opinion to someone I don't know very well.		
34.	Interrupting someone to ask him or her to repeat something I didn't hear clearly.		
35.	Contradicting someone when I think I might hurt him or her by doing so.		
36.	Telling someone that he or she has disappointed me or let me down.		
37.	Asking someone to leave me alone.		
38.	Telling a friend or co-worker that he or she has done a good job.		
39.	Telling someone he or she has made a good point in a discussion.		
40.	Telling someone I have enjoyed talking with him or her.		
41.	Complimenting someone on his or her skill or creativity.[3]		

As you begin to share yourself more, make a list of what you feel you need to do and want to do. Here is a sample list from a woman.

1. Tell my husband in a calm voice that I am upset over something he failed to do for me last week.
2. Let my Bible-study leader know that I would like her not to call on me for the next two weeks while I work out my responses and how to handle those requests for answers.
3. When I am with other people, I let others do what they want and go where they want. I would like to express my preference.
4. Be able to say no immediately to phone solicitors.
5. Let my neighbors know that their dog barks all night long when they leave it alone.
6. Be able to say no to pushy sales people and not give reasons.
7. To come into a group and say hello to at least three people. To engage one in conversation.

As you begin to do this, it is important to prepare in advance and rate your feelings of comfort (on a scale of 1 to 5) and how skillful you were (on a scale of 1 to 5). A 1 is very uncomfortable and not very skillful. A 3 is the middle ground, and 5 means very comfortable and very skillful. There is a good reason for keeping track of your behavior. It gives you the opportunity to see how your behavior changes over a period of time.

The best way to break out of your old patterns and develop both the confidence and skill needed for your new response to life is to practice *social skill imagery*. This is something you can accomplish in the privacy of your own mind. You can try various responses and refine them. You can make all the mistakes you want to inwardly. No one will know about your refinement process. You can create any type of situation in your head.

Take one or two of the actual situations on the list you just made. Choose either the two that are the easiest or the two that are likely to occur the soonest. This assures you of some success immediately and helps you become better prepared for those that are most likely to occur. As you begin your imagery practice sessions, spend at least fifteen minutes a day. Have your practice sessions in a room free from interruptions. Lying down on the bed or the living room couch may work for you. Take the phone off the hook, be sure the television is off, and if needed, put a DO NOT DISTURB sign on the door. Especially at the start of this new approach, you need to create a quiet practice environment for yourself.

Select one of your own personal concerns, close your eyes, and imagine an actual scene. Using technicolor in your image, try to imagine the location, who is there, where you are in the scene, what you and others are wearing, and so on. Picture the events leading up to the moment when you want to begin behaving in a new manner. Create a picture of the situation in your own imagination as though it were an actual photograph. Now that you have it in mind in stop action, make it into a videotape. Imagine what each person is doing and saying. Picture as clearly as you can your new behavior. See yourself doing and saying what you would like to and what you will feel good about.

Be sure that you visualize yourself speaking and behaving with confidence and with no hesitancy. You are in control, and you are not offensive in any way. See yourself responding in such a way that when finished you are quite satisfied with yourself. It does not have to be a production; it can be brief and simple.

As you do this, imagine that you feel the touch of a supportive hand upon your shoulder. You do not need to turn around to look at who is touching you in this manner. You realize that standing and moving with you each step of the way is Jesus Christ. He is there, caring for you, loving you, and giving to you His support and strength. You are learning to respond differently, not out of your strength and ability alone but through His power and presence. Jesus believes in your ability to accomplish this. He wants you to be a new person, to develop the potential God has endowed you with, and to be more effective for the cause of Christ.

Now imagine what happens after you make your statement.

What do the other people say and do? Be sure that you imagine positive effects of your new behavior and do not slip back into your negative worrisome pattern of anticipation. On occasion, you can imagine that others do not respond as you would like, because occasionally they won't. But this will not happen nearly as much as you fear. Actually you are not really trying to change the behavior or comments of other people; you are learning to handle situations yourself in a more positive manner.

Once you have completed the scene, go back and play it again. This time change some of the details. You might want to change your comments a bit or alter what leads up to the situation. Go through this sequence several times and be sure to change it from time to time. Always show in your videotape what leads up to your new positive and satisfying behavior and the response (usually positive) you receive from others.

Here is an example from a college girl who was concerned about her lack of interaction with other college students at her church. She would either arrive at her meeting a few minutes late, which allowed her to avoid interaction with others, or if she did arrive early she would head for a corner of the room and pretty much isolate herself. Here is a synopsis of the sequence.

FIRST SEQUENCE
Photograph. I am at my college-age class at church. I have arrived early, and there are about twenty-five people in the room. Some of them are talking in groups, and others are standing and talking in groups of two. A few are just standing by not doing anything.

Movie or videotape: I see myself walking into the room. Some of the others notice me and look my way. Others are engrossed in their own conversations. A couple of people say hello to me but continue on conversing with the others. I walk a bit farther into the room, feeling a little anxious and hesitant, but I decide to approach someone in conversation.

Social interaction: I walk up to two other girls and say

"Hi. I've seen you at a couple of my classes at school and also noticed you here at church. It seems as if we have a couple of things in common. I was wondering if you would like to go out for coffee after class." Response, "You're right. We do end up meeting in several classes. Why don't you sit here? There's an extra chair, and the coffee sounds like a great idea. I'm dragging from being out late, and I didn't have a chance to get any. Thanks for asking." I feel the hand on my shoulder as I begin sharing, realizing that I am not sharing out of my own strength. I visualize Jesus standing there with me.

Now let's take one of the situations from the woman's list on p. 163. The first item on her list had to do with wanting to tell her husband that she was a bit upset over something he had failed to do the week before.

Photograph: You are with your husband. You are sitting in the family room after dinner. The television is off. It is a pleasant time. Both of you are a bit tired after a busy day, and you are relaxing.

Movie or videotape: You see yourself in the same situation, and now you are engaging in some light talk about the day's events. You talk about a few things concerning the house. There has been no conflict or serious discussion up to this point, and both of you are enjoying the time. You are thinking about sharing with him what had occurred the previous week. You are a little anxious, but you can share it properly. So you begin.

Social interaction: "Honey, last week you mentioned you would be able to clean up a section of the garage for me, so I could use that area for storage. I was counting on that before the weekend, but somehow it didn't get done. I was a little disappointed, but I would still like to have it done. Would you be able to give me a definite time you could do it this week?" As you do this, imagine the hand of Jesus Christ upon your shoulder, supporting you and giving you strength.

Response: Your husband looks a bit surprised and then slaps his hand to his forehead. "Oh, boy! You're right. I completely forgot to do that. I guess I'm not looking forward to it. But I said I would, and it's important to you. Yup, I'll have it done by Saturday evening. Thanks for letting me know."

To help you learn the art of visual imagery, you might want to try it in writing first to get the feel of it. You don't have to write an entire book, but be sure that the major images, words, and sequences are there. If you feel satisfied with your creation of scenes, set a schedule for practicing it this week—at least fifteen minutes a day. Use two of the situations on your own list. Do this for a week.

Imagery practice will give you the skills you are looking for as well as a greater belief in your own capabilities. Naturally the next step will be trying your skills in the world of reality. You may feel anxious, awkward, embarrassed, and amateurish. Give yourself permission to feel that way. This is normal. The more you learn to express yourself, the more you will understand that this new approach is the new you! Don't wait for a situation to occur by chance but, instead, plan some opportunities for you to be more socially active. Try to arrange those that hold the least amount of risk and have the greatest opportunity for success. Rehearse as fully as you possibly can. Do not plan for perfection, for this hinders your progress. Gradual growth and progress will be a major step for you.

After you have been practicing various situations for two weeks, go back over your rating form of comfort and skill and rate yourself again. If you feel comfortable about your progress, your imagery practice sessions can occur just about anywhere. You can do it while riding in a car or bus or even during a break at work. Learning to be flexible and spontaneous with this new approach will give you a greater degree of confidence. Before long you will be able to respond positively right on the spot when situations occur.

You do not have to remain paralyzed because of one of those habits held over from your past. Some physical paralysis, such as that caused by polio or a spinal cord injury, offers little hope of recovery. However, paralysis because of fear, insecurities, and an overwhelming need for approval can be healed. You can, like the man at the pool, stand up and walk, and carry your bed—the symbol of his helplessness—with you. Why do you suppose Jesus told him to take his bed with him? Could it be that He was telling the man that he would have no more use for it? It was a reminder of his past life, and Jesus was saying, "Take it away, for you have no more need for this." He was not allowing the man the possibility of a relapse. It is so easy to doubt the permanency of change in our lives. We want to keep one hand holding onto our past support system.

The man might have asked, "What if I wake up tomorrow and I can't walk again? What if this doesn't last? I had better prepare in case I become paralyzed again."

Jesus was saying, "Your past is gone, and you are to live in the newness of the life I have given you."

Emotional paralysis is not a permanent malady; it can be cured. Not only will you be able to walk, you will walk without a limp. You can put away your crutches and pallet if you let Jesus Christ teach you to walk.

11

Treating Your Wounds

Using this book, you have discovered your unnecessary baggage, begun to reparent yourself, and started to grow toward freedom. But what happens to you when emotional wounds still seem to hinder your progress? Let's look at a few of those that may interfere with your life journey.

Identifying the Wounds

We usually think of wounds occurring in battles or during fights. In our mind's eye we picture soldiers crawling, limping, or struggling to move. Wounds limit you. They diminish your capabilities. But they will heal if they are treated correctly.

Some of these emotional wounds include discouragement, a sense of failure, despair, grief, guilt, self-rejection, and self-pity. Those of us who have emotional wounds may react in one of four ways:

1. By blocking or repressing our emotions and living life only with our minds.
2. By living life based upon our emotions and being over-sensitive.
3. By becoming suspicious or paranoid.
4. By living continually with sadness or depression.

A person who has been wounded emotionally often manifests his wounds in loneliness. When you were a child, one of the first things you should have learned was to trust others. Trust was essential, because you were completely dependent upon others for every function in life; that was the only way you could survive. But if your caretakers were not loving or trustworthy and were inconsistent in their care of you, you soon became cautious about them. You became convinced that not only could other people not be trusted, but they were actually out to "get you" or "do you in." You learned to be careful and, eventually, suspicious. You became a lonely person.

Loneliness is a prison. You may be with other people, but you still feel alone. You deliberately cut yourself off from other people, leaving yourself emotionally isolated. You become suspicious. You cannot take other people at face value. When their closeness and intimacy become too threatening, you choose isolation as the lesser of two evils. And of course you blame other people for your isolation; it is their untrustworthiness that drove you to isolation.

Psalms 142:4 graphically describes the feeling of a lonely person: "Look to the right and see: For there is no one who regards me; There is no escape for me; No one cares for my soul" (NAS). Not only is loneliness the feeling that you are cut off from other people, deserted, and banished from their company, it is also a breakdown in emotional giving and receiving between people. Loneliness is frequently self-inflicted. It is a state of continual wounding.

Repressing Emotions

One form of isolation and loneliness is to block our emotions and feelings. Feelings are the way we sense being alive. They are our reaction to the world around us. Without an awareness of our feelings, we have little interaction with life.

Some people retreat into their intellects to hide from their feelings. There is less pain with thoughts and words than there is with feelings. They don't really trust their feelings anyway, because feelings can be very unstable. Emotional injuries are greater than any intellectual wounds, and they drain us of hope and energy.

So they learn to protect themselves with their minds and become fearful and withdrawn from others. Their capacity to give and receive love is limited. They either become more demanding or more suspicious of others. Some people have such a tight lid on their minds that certain emotions are never even allowed to develop. A person's mind can actually prevent him from feeling emotions of awe, love, peace, joy, and tenderness.

Being Oversensitive

Emotional maturity means recognizing and accepting what has happened in your life without seeking to place blame or regretting your past. It means living in the present and continuing to move forward. Many times a person's chronological age does not match his emotional age. A person who was affirmed as a child has an easier time becoming emotionally mature. If you were not affirmed as a child, you will have to work toward emotional maturity.

The lack of affirmation from others prevents you from developing a sense of your own worth, value, or goodness, which, in turn, causes you to be fearful and untrusting. You have trouble opening up to the world around you. You even have trouble opening yourself to God. Your emotions remain undeveloped because you did not receive proper nourishment as a child. This results in your being oversensitive or closed emotionally. Both are wounds.

The oversensitive person who lives his life based upon emotions chooses a life of uncertainty. Continually listening to his emotions leaves him with doubts. He does not feel at ease and he wonders about the thoughts, feelings, and reactions of others. He tries to "check out" what others think and feel about him, but even when he is affirmed, he still has lingering doubts.

Inner uncertainty seeks constant assurance and affirmation.

The oversensitive person wears his emotions on his sleeve. He is easily hurt. Even a simple difference of opinion or minor disagreement can lead to bewilderment or depression. He is continually alienated and isolated from other people. His present feelings are still influenced by feeling memories of the past.

If the pain of the past has not been settled, we do not fully live the feelings of the present. Unfortunately, in our attempts to block the pain of the past, we also block out the pleasures of the past. Even though we may have negative memories, we also have positive memories that should not be negated. Positive memories create the optimist within us; negative memories bring out the pessimist.

In earlier centuries, when people owed money and could not pay their bills, they were thrown into debtors' prison. Unfortunately, this action punished both the debtor and the one to whom he owed money. For while the person was in prison, he could hardly earn any money to pay off the debt.

Many of us live today in a debtors' prison. As long as the emotional debts of the past exist, the interest accrues and the indebtedness increases. If we proceed through life unwilling to trust and love for fear of loss and pain, life becomes narrower and encumbered with debt. When we are finally able to risk loving, and when trusting begins, life becomes happier and more fulfilled.

From time to time all of us have episodes of emotional debt when we trap certain feelings inside and block off our capacity to feel. But the more we create a barrier around our feelings, the more constricted we become. Hurt is a part of life. Being let down is a part of life. Being rejected is a part of life. We live in an imperfect world, so why should we expect so much consistency from other people?

Getting out of emotional debt involves accepting yourself and others with all of our shortcomings. It means reaching out and trying and trusting. If you are guarding your emotional life, you are under continual stress, and you are not seeing life as it really is. No matter how terrible your past experiences have been, you need to be able to feel and not just to think. A nontrusting person lives with a consistent low level of fear. It is like walking around with a soft hum in your ears, reminding you to be cautious and wary.

What is it you are afraid of? Is it really fear that keeps you so closed up, or is it something else? What is the worst possible thing that could happen to you if you opened your life to your feelings? Would it be any worse than what you are experiencing now? If you are lonely, share your feelings with someone. If you are hurt, let others know. If you are angry, say so in a positive way. If you are sad, tell someone. If you want to live life in the present, with hope for the future, accept what has happened in the past, for it cannot be changed.

Becoming Suspicious

The ability to trust means that you allow deep relationships to occur. But there are many people today who find it difficult to trust anyone. *Suspicious* is the key word of their lives. When you do not trust others, it indicates that you are vulnerable. A persistent low-grade or high-grade fear is your form of fever. In its extreme form you feel (and really believe) that someone may be watching you, that others do not like you, no matter what they say, that your spouse cares about other people more than you.

There are various degrees of suspicion, ranging from the belief that other people are out to get you or that someone is watching your home, to the belief that other people can read your mind. The boss's door is closed, and you are dead certain he is talking to someone else about you. A friend stops talking on the phone when you come in, and you're sure that he was talking about you. Three other employees are sitting at lunch laughing, and you know who they are laughing about.

If you tend to be suspicious, you are a person who has something on your mind. You look at the world with a fixed, preoccupying expectation. You search and search in order to confirm this expectation. It is difficult for you to abandon your suspicion or your plan of action based on it. Rational arguments do not really help. And often, if someone tries to talk you out of your thoughts, you become suspicious of that person also.

A suspicious person does not ignore information and facts. He examines them very carefully, but with a prejudice. His intelligence, keenness, and sharpness of attention are not based on realistic judgment but are instruments of bias. He has acute, narrow attention in relationships.

Being overly suspicious did not just happen. The seeds for this response to life were planted probably very early in your life, and you are not only harvesting that crop but planting a bigger one. Every time you give in to a suspicious thought or feeling, you may gain some immediate relief, but you strengthen its hold upon you.

Oversuspicion is a feeling of jeopardy. You especially care about something you possess, and you feel very vulnerable about it. You also may feel that the reason you might lose it stems from some real or apparent defect within you. Because of this structure it is very easy to act upon your feelings. Every time you act out of fear you reinforce the fear.

Some examples of oversuspicion are: checking and rechecking the locks on a door; looking around to see if someone is watching you; tearing open an envelope you just sealed to see if you signed your check; reentering the house to see if you turned off the stove; checking your wallet several times while shopping, to make sure it is still there. It does pay to be careful and check yourself. But the oversuspicious person commits acts of *unwarranted* self-protection.

The air of suspicion extends to our imagined shortcomings. Dr. George Weinberg tells the story of a man who applied for a job with an advertising firm. John wasn't completely truthful about his past experience. He had a few jobs in the past, and he told this new company that he had actually written copy for a successful ad campaign. In reality he had only typed the ad copy. He was afraid he wouldn't get this important job unless they were impressed with his background. He really wanted the job. John's resulting problems stemmed both from sin and the fear his mind created.

The company was impressed with his application, and he got the job. But then he began to wonder why he was hired. Was it because of his ability, or his references, or because of writing that one successful ad copy? What if his new job was based upon that one lie? This meant he could be in for some real problems if his new employer discovered the lie. This was the best job he had ever had. It paid well, his friends were impressed, and he was able to move into a better apartment.

As his suspicions grew he became more and more uncomfortable at work. What if his boss found out? What if his boss started to question his performance? His boss could be expecting some high-quality copy such as he supposedly produced at his former job. Each day that John went to work, there was a bit of fear that he would be found out for what he feels he is—a fraud.

His original lie began to direct his activities at work. Because he was worried about being fired, he came in early, skipped lunch, stayed late, and worked harder than anyone else. He flattered his superiors. Each time he acted in a way to safeguard his job, he was reinforcing his oversuspicious tendencies and his fear that doing the best job he could would not be enough to keep this job.

The lie kept plaguing him, and his mind began to work overtime. What if his boss met someone from the place he used to work? What if someone who didn't like him at his former job called his boss to talk about him? Every time the boss got a phone call or read a letter and looked John's way, John's stomach did a tumble. He was sure that other people were telling the boss he had lied! He even resorted to looking at his employer's mail after hours to see if anyone had written about him. He asked the boss's secretary if his employer had received any calls about him. None of these actions sufficed, however. They kept increasing his fear and suspicion.[1]

Whenever you act on unwarranted fear, trying to make it go away, you increase your fear and strengthen your belief that you must take these and other precautions. Becoming oversuspicious actually becomes easier and easier. You allow your mind to build a false view of life for you. This pattern of living, which had its origins years ago, now controls and dominates you.

Being paranoid or suspicious is paralyzed thinking, but you *can* change. If you are ready to admit that this is your pattern and that it is not the best way to live, here is what to do.

First of all, when you find yourself doing something to protect yourself, stop immediately. Try to determine what you are trying to accomplish with your action. What is your goal? Are you achieving your goal? Do you feel better now or worse? How will you feel in a few days or even a few hours? Are your fears less now or worse? If you are honest, you will probably say the action did not help. Why? Because each behavior reinforces your belief that these behaviors are really necessary.

Second, stop yourself *before* you follow through with your behavior. If you have been checking the locks and or trying to find out what people think of you, stop before you finish the action. How do you feel? By denying your basic impulse, you cause it to grow or enlarge. This method is called magnification. It will bring your fear into focus. Pay attention to all of your thoughts and feelings. Let them emerge. Write them down so you can face them squarely.

The purpose of both of these suggestions is to find the behaviors that reinforce your fears and to stop doing them. This will actually weaken your impulse to behave in this way and will also weaken your tendency toward suspicious thinking. But at first you will probably feel worse and will try to talk yourself into acting on the impulse. You are *not* going to lose whatever it is you are afraid of losing. You are worrying, and your interpretation of what is about to occur is not rooted in fact. It is an old message from ancient history that is still operating.

Here are some additional steps to follow to help you recognize behavior that actually reinforces your tendency to be suspicious.

1.   In your relationships with friends and trusted relatives, do not hide feelings or situations from them because you are

afraid that it will ruin your relationship. Whatever it is
that you are tempted to hide from the other person, don't.
It will simply make the problem seem larger. You will
begin to wonder about the depth of a relationship that
leads to fear of discovery. Many Christians hide their depression from other Christians, because they fear they will
not be accepted.

2. Don't ask for reassurance from others. Even if you tend to
be uncertain of your relationship or friendship, don't ask
if they like you or accept you. If you act upon that impulse, it will only make it increase, not go away. If you
ask, do you think you will actually believe the answer of
reassurance and affirmation anyway?

3. Don't accuse other people of negative thoughts or actions
toward you that you have probably imposed upon them
anyway. It will only make you more suspicious of others.

4. Don't try to correct other people's behavior. If you do, you
are just showing your fear of what people might do to you.
If you tell your friend, "Don't forget to buy me a
Christmas gift," or, "Don't be angry at me," you are an-
ticipating what someone else is going to do or not do. You
are thinking the worst and trying to correct it before it
occurs. Trust others instead of trying to control their behavior or check up on them.

5. If you have a driving impulse for immediate information
and usually search it out, don't. If you wonder what your
friend meant by a particular comment, don't call and ask
for an explanation. If your boss tells you he wants to discuss something with you tomorrow, don't hint or pester
him to find out what it is about. Let it ride and realize that
you can function without having all the answers. If you
can stop trying to control your life so much, you can begin
to trust and respond differently to life around you.[2]

All of us have wounds. Some are visible, and some are not.
Recently I watched a newscast in which the life of a young
man was presented. He was born with deformed arms and

hands and with one leg missing below the knee. These permanent wounds could have easily limited his life and experiences. Yet he has won dozens of trophies and awards for his tennis playing, and he is now a tennis coach. He speaks to large groups of young people across the country. As he shared his life before one group I heard him say, "We are all handicapped. The only difference is that you can see my handicap. I cannot see yours." His handicap did not limit him. Hidden handicaps, however, do limit us. Facing them, sharing them, and treating them gives us a new beginning.

Living With Depression

Another type of wound we need to talk about is depression. Some people live in a constant state of sadness. Occasional journeys into this realm are normal and give depth and balance to our lives. Sadness can cause us to become more contemplative, serious, thoughtful, and grateful and give us a new purpose for living life to the fullest. But constant sadness takes the sunshine and delight out of lives. Loss brings about sadness, which can move into depression.

Over the years I have learned to handle a particular type of loss. Our son, Matthew, is profoundly mentally retarded. Chronologically he is seventeen years old, but mentally he is only about fifteen months. We have learned a great deal about ourselves, about life, and the faithfulness of God through having Matt. We understand and accept him for what his name means, "God's gift." But in our odyssey with Matthew there are still occasional times when we deeply feel his loss and ours.

Recently a friend and I met for an early morning racket-ball game. He shared with me how he had taken his six-year-old son on an overnight camping trip. They slept in a tent, made their breakfast over a fire, and played together in the stream. As he went into detail, sharing his excitement and delight, part of me was happy with him, another part was very uncomfortable. I even had feelings of *I wish he would stop telling me this.*

I soon realized what was occurring with me. I was once again feeling the sense of loss. I wished that I had been able to have those experiences with my son, but I never would. The time was past, never to be retrieved. Matthew's limited capabilities would not allow this experience to be one he and I would ever share together. I experienced the loss one more time, and a sense of sadness was with me for the entire day. But it was an experience that once again God used as I shared it with a client to help him begin to feel and live. I also shared this with Joyce, my wife, and it was a time of our drawing closer together. The sadness lifted the next day, and I had changed because of that brief experience. It is now another one of the memories that make up my past but gives a deeper meaning and depth to life.

Wounded people are sad or depressed people. And this sadness or depression can recreate and control their vision, for depression distorts our perception of life.

Each of us perceives life from our backlog of experiences, because our memories are always with us. Our perceptions happen automatically, and we believe that what we perceive is the real world.

Father Richard F. Berg and Christine McCartney describe our ability to perceive as similar to a camera. Photographers can alter the image of reality through the use of various lenses or filters. Thus what the camera records may not be an accurate view of the world. A wide-angle lens gives you a much wider panorama, but the objects in the picture appear much more distant and smaller. A telephoto lens has a much narrower and selective view of life. It can focus on a beautiful flower, but at the same time it shuts out the rest of the garden. A normal lens will capture happy and smiling people, but those same people seen through a fish-eye lens become distorted and unreal. Filters can blur reality, break images into pieces, bring darkness into a lighted scene, even create a mist.

Like the lenses and filters on a camera, our perception of the world can become distorted. Depression focuses upon the darker portions of life and takes away the warmth, action, and joy from a scene. A photographer is aware of the distortion that he is creating as he switches lens. The depressed person, however, is not that aware of the distortion in his perception of reality. When we are depressed, we are practically blind, without knowing it. And the greater the intensity of our depression, the greater the distortion.[3]

What do we distort? We distort life itself, causing it to lose its excitement and purpose. We distort the image of God. We see Him as far away and uncaring, as though a tremendous gulf were separating us from Him. And we also distort our own view of ourselves. Our worth, value, and abilities vanish along with hope.

Depression is a symptom, a disease, and a reaction. It is a warning system (a symptom) calling our attention to the fact that something is wrong. Psychotic depression is also a disease, an illness. And depression is a reaction to life, especially a reaction to the many losses we experience throughout our lives. There is always a reason for depression.

Many Christians have the mistaken idea that it is wrong for a Christian to be depressed. If it is a sin to be depressed, then the prophet Jeremiah must have been the chief among sinners, for much of what he wrote came while he was in a depressed state. We were created with the capacity to become depressed when certain factors are present in our lives. Depression can be a welcome symptom warning us that we are moving into deep water, if we are willing to accept it as such. It can remind us that we cannot rely upon our own resources. We need to move back to God and His resources. It can be a short-term protective device that gives us a breather from stress and tension, allowing us time to recover. Depression is a warning system that God has created for us. However, God does not allow us to be depressed as a form of punishment. He has taken care of our punishment on the cross.

But we must not remain in our depression and choose it as a constant way of life. When we are in a light state of depression or sadness, we can choose to heed its warning and make some changes. Or we can linger too long and allow it to take up permanent residence in our lives.

Causes of Depression

Among the causes of depression are those issues from our past that still influence us. One of the major issues is deprivation.

An infant child is dependent upon his mother for physical and emotional care and for survival. His mother's warmth, nourishment, and gentle fondling convey to the child a message of love and security. When he has a need, mother responds. Mother is faithful to his cries, and thus the child learns to trust. Faithful mothering builds trust.

But what happens when the child is repeatedly ignored or his mother responds, but without love? The child soon learns that Mother, and even other people, cannot be trusted. He begins to feel neglected and unappreciated. He does not understand why his world appears untrustworthy, undependable, and unloving. These early experiences develop a low frustration level within him. Who can he trust? Feelings of resentment and anger that develop as seedlings in these early years continue to develop under the surface on into adulthood. They make it difficult for him to forgive. His experience with mistrust often predisposes him to become depression prone later in life.

In depression there is the feeling of loss, hopelessness, and as Richard Berg and Christine McCartney state, a "spiritual sadness."

> Sadness is a wound deep within the spiritual self-concept. It often produces a considerable suffering for the depressed person and may be viewed as a "tree that thrives in darkness." The twin roots of this tree—(1) the belief that one is unloved, with the perplexing inability to forgive (resentment), and (2) the belief that one is unlovable, with resistance to accepting forgiveness (perfectionism)—distort one's perception of the present and dims one's expectations for the future. This "tree" of darkness cannot

flourish in the light which God's unconditional and healing love brings. The Lord longs to heal spiritual sadness by leading us out of darkness: he brings glad tidings to the lowly, heals the brokenhearted, proclaims liberty to captives and release to those who are prisoners (Is. 61:1).

In fact, Jesus said of himself, "I am the light of the world. No follower of mine shall wander in the dark; he shall have the light of life" (Jn. 8:12).

The psalmist exults in God's healing, loving presence: "You indeed, O Lord, give light to my lamp; O my God, you brighten the darkness about me" (Ps. 18:28).[4]

The wound of sadness often leads to guilt over one's imperfections. It is no surprise that many who struggle with depression are perfectionists. They set standards for themselves so high they become easy targets for failure. Soon they feel as if a giant weight has been dropped on them.

Jesus responds to all of us who feel guilty over our imperfections by offering us forgiveness and release from the burdens we carry. "Come to Me, all who are weary and heavy-laden, and I will give you rest. Take My yoke upon you, and learn from Me, for I am gentle and humble in heart; and you shall find rest for your souls. For My yoke is easy, and My load is light" (Matthew 11:28–30 NAS).

The depressed person feels empty and without hope. He believes he is unloved, that nobody really cares about him. The psalmist describes such feelings when he says:

O Lord, the God of my salvation, I have cried out by day and in the night before Thee. . . . For my soul has had enough troubles, and my life has drawn near to Sheol. I am reckoned among those who go down to the pit; I have become like a man without strength, Forsaken among the dead, Like the slain who lie in the grave, Whom Thou dost remember no more, And they are cut off from Thy hand. . . . I was afflicted and about to die from my youth on; I suffer Thy terrors; I am overcome.

Psalms 88:1, 3–5, 15 NAS

Jesus responds with these comforting facts: "The thief comes only to steal, and kill, and destroy; I came that they might have life, and might have it abundantly" (John 10:10 NAS). "These things I have spoken to you, that My joy may be in you, and that your joy may be made full" (John 15:11 NAS).

The depressed person has great doubts about himself and about whether or not he is loved. These doubts can soon develop into resentment. If we do not express and deal with this resentment, it simply feeds our depression. The Word of God offers ample evidence that we are indeed loved:

> For God so loved the world, that He gave His only begotten Son, that whoever believes in Him should not perish, but have eternal life.
>
> John 3:16 NAS

> What do you think? If any man has a hundred sheep, and one of them has gone astray, does he not leave the ninety-nine on the mountains and go and search for the one that is straying? And if it turns out that he finds it, truly I say to you, he rejoices over it more than over the ninety-nine which have not gone astray. Thus it is not the will of your Father who is in heaven that one of these little ones perish.
>
> Matthew 18:12–14 NAS

> I am the good shepherd; the good shepherd lays down His life for the sheep . . .
>
> John 10:11 NAS

Chuck Swindoll offers some words of comfort for those of us who are living with the scars of past sins or failures.

> Although you have confessed and forsaken those ugly, bitter days, you can't seem to erase the backwash. Sometimes when you're alone the past slips up from behind like a freak ocean wave and overwhelms you. The scab is jarred loose. The wound stays inflamed and tender and you wonder if it will *ever* go away. Although it is unknown

to others, you live in the fear of being found out . . . and
rejected.

It was Amy Carmichael who once helped heal a wound
within me and turn it into a scar of beauty instead of dis-
grace. I share with you her words:

NO SCAR?

Hast thou no scar?
No hidden scar on foot, or side, or hand?
I hear thee sung as mighty in the land,
I hear them hail thy bright ascendant star,
Hast thou no scar?

Hast thou no wound?
Yet I was wounded by the archers, spent,
Leaned Me against a tree to die; and rent
By ravening beasts that compassed Me, I swooned;
Hast thou no wound?

No wound, no scar?
Yet, as the Master shall the servant be,
And, pierced are the feet that follow Me;
But thine are whole; can he have followed far
Who has no wound nor scar?

Tucked away in a quiet corner of every life are wounds
and scars. If they were not there, we would need no Physician. Nor would we need one another.[5]

If you are stuck in life, feeling unhappy, isolated, overly
sensitive, suspicious, or depressed, there is hope in the healing
power of Jesus Christ. Here are some exercises to follow, which
can start you on the road to wholeness:

1. What is it from your past that is still influencing the way
    you act and think today? Some people object to spending
    time looking at the past. Certainly too much time spent
    looking back can be unhealthy. However, in order to
    move toward wholeness, we need to identify the cause of

our wounds. We are not digging about in the cemetery of
our minds, looking for emotional ghosts to come back and
haunt us. Rather we are looking for half-filled graves that
need to be filled in.

2.   If you were a trusting person, how would you respond to
     others? Are you living today in the distrust of your past? It
     is difficult to live in two worlds.

3.   If you were emotionally open to sharing your love, hurts,
     and joy, how do you visualize yourself responding to
     other people? Spend a few quiet minutes picturing your-
     self responding in new and positive ways. Each day take
     one small step toward becoming the new you.

4.   If you were not sad or depressed right now, what would
     you be doing with your life? Describe this in detail on a
     piece of paper. What one thing could you begin doing that
     would move you toward a new life of hope and joy?

5.   Describe on a piece of paper the details of your sadness
     and depression. Then write down what you do each day
     from the time you get up until you go to bed.

     When my patients who are depressed explain to me
     how they use their time, I usually discover that much of
     what they are doing is actually keeping the sadness and
     depression alive in their lives. "If I were living my life as
     you are living yours," I say to them, "I would probably
     feel worse than you do! How do you keep yourself from
     being even sadder and more depressed than you are? You
     must have a lot going for you that you aren't even aware
     of. Let's discover what it is, so you can use it even more."

Who can heal your wounds? Self-examination and commitment to growth are important. The cause of some of your
wounds may be so hidden you will need the help of a professional counselor before you can move ahead. But regardless of
where you go for help, Jesus Christ is the source of your healing, because He is also the source of the hope you have as
God's child. Becoming fully aware of the eternal significance
of your adoption into your heavenly Father's family (Gala-

tians 4:4, 5) gives you a priceless key that just fits the lock of your life. Place the key in this lock, turn it, and the lock springs open!

As you remove the lock and open the door to your inner self, restrictions, fetters, chains, anchors and feelings of hopelessness drop away. Opening the lock gives you the opportunity to look objectively at who you are today, at the influence of the past, and what you would like to do with your life in the future. Because of the Holy Spirit prompting and reminding you of your adoptive status (Romans 8:15, 16), you can now begin to take risks. You can step out in faith in what God will do to nurture and discipline the immature inner child of the past and empower you to grow up into the mature adult He has always planned for you to be.

Dr. Lloyd Ogilvie has influenced my life for many years. His insightful words help us come to the fitting conclusion of our journey to make peace with the past:

> We all need power. We need an inner energizing of our minds and wills. We were meant to be recreated to be like Jesus. We cannot do it on our own, but He is able! The indwelling Christ, the power at work in us, infuses the tissues of our brains with a vivid picture of the person we can become. Then He guides each decision and discernment of our wills. He shows us how we are to act and react as new creatures. Our depleted energies are engendered with strength. We actually have supernatural power to think, act, and respond with infused capacities.[6]

Source Notes

Introduction

1. A. W. Tozer, *The Knowledge of the Holy* (New York: Harper & Row, 1961), p. 107.

Chapter 1

1. W. Hugh Missildine, *Your Inner Child of the Past* (New York: Simon & Schuster, 1968), p. 4.
2. Howard Halpern, *Cutting Loose: A Guide to Adult Terms With Your Parents* (New York: Bantam, 1978), p. 3.
3. W. Hugh Missildine and Lawrence Galton, *Your Inner Conflicts* (New York: Simon & Schuster, 1974), p. 17.

Chapter 2

1. W. Hugh Missildine, *Your Inner Child of the Past* (New York: Simon & Schuster, 1968).
2. Adapted from Frederic F. Flack, *The Secret Strength of Depression* (New York: J. B. Lippincott, 1975).

Chapter 3

1. Henri J. M. Nouwen, *The Living Reminder: Service and Prayer in Memory of Jesus Christ* (New York: Seabury Press, 1977), p. 19.
2. Ibid, p. 22.

3. Matthew L. Linn and D. Linn, *Healing of Memories* (Ramsey, N. J.: Paulist Press, 1974), pp. 11, 12.

4. Lloyd John Ogilvie, *God's Will in Your Life* (Eugene, Ore.: Harvest House, 1982), p. 136.

5. J. I. Packer, *Knowing God* (Downers Grove, Ill.: InterVarsity, 1973), p. 32.

6. Ogilvie, *God's Will in Your Life,* pp. 144, 145.

Chapter 4

1. Norman Vincent Peale, *Positive Imaging* (Old Tappan, N. J.: Fleming H. Revell, 1982), p. 17.

2. Ibid.

3. John W. Drakeford, *The Awesome Power of the Healing Thought* (Nashville: Broadman, 1981), p. 120. All rights reserved. Used by permission.

4. Alan Richardson, *Mental Imagery* (New York: Springer Pub., 1969), p. 56.

5. W. Timothy Gallwey, *The Inner Game of Tennis* (New York: Random House, 1979), p. 59.

6. Mike Samuels and Nancy Samuels, *Seeing With the Mind's Eye* (New York: Random House, 1975), p. 169.

Chapter 5

1. Lewis B. Smedes, *Forgive and Forget* (New York: Harper & Row, 1984), p. 118.

2. The approach described in relinquishing resentments and forgiving others is used, in varying forms, by many therapists and ministers, including the following: Matthew L. Linn and D. Linn, *Healing of Memories* (Ramsey, N.J.: Paulist Press, 1974), *see* pp. 94–96; Dennis and Matthew Linn, *Healing Life's Hurts* (Ramsey, N.J.: Paulist Press, 1977), *see* pp. 218 f.; Howard Halpern, *Cutting Loose: A Guide to Adult Terms With Your Parents* (New York: Bantam, 1978), pp. 212 f. (The empty-chair technique that is described in Gestalt literature is described in this section); David L. Luecke, *The Relationship Manual* (Columbia, Md.: Relationship Institute, 1981), *see* pp. 88–91; *see also* past issues of "The Journal of Christian Healing," published by the Institute of Christian Healing, 103 Dudley Avenue, Narbelk, Penn. 19072.

3. Lama Foundation, *Be Here Now* (New York: Crown Publications, 1971), p. 55.

4. Adapted from Howard M. Halpern, *Cutting Loose: A Guide to Adult Terms With Your Parents* (New York: Bantam, 1978) pp. 24, 25.

5. Joyce Landorf, *Irregular People* (Waco, Tex.: Word, 1982) pp. 61, 62.

6. Lloyd John Ogilvie, *God's Best for My Life* (Eugene, Ore.: Harvest House, 1981), p. 1.

7. Lewis B. Smedes, "Forgiveness: The Power to Change the Past," *Christianity Today,* 7 January 1983, p. 26.

8. Ogilvie, *God's Best,* p. 9.

9. Smedes, *Forgive and Forget,* p. 37.

Chapter 6

1. W. Hugh Missildine, *Your Inner Child of the Past* (New York: Simon & Schuster, 1968), p. 59.

2. Howard M. Halpern, *Cutting Loose: A Guide to Adult Terms With Your Parents* (New York: Bantam, 1977), p. 126.

3. J. I. Packer, *Knowing God* (Downers Grove, Ill.: InterVarsity, 1973), p. 37.

4. Joseph R. Cooke, *Free for the Taking* (Old Tappan, N. J.: Fleming H. Revell, 1975), p. 29.

5. Maurice Wagner, *The Sensation of Being Somebody* (Grand Rapids: Zondervan, 1975), pp. 164–167.

6. Halpern, *Cutting Loose,* p. 128.

Chapter 7

1. Jane B. Burka and Lenora M. Yuen, *Procrastination* (Menlo Park, Calif.: Addison-Wesley, 1980), p. 28.

2. David Burns, *Feeling Good: The New Mood Therapy* (New York: New American Library, 1981), p. 313.

3. John Robert Clarke, *The Importance of Being Imperfect* (New York: David McKay, 1981), p. 11.

4. Burns, *Feeling Good,* pp. 319, 320.

Chapter 9

1. W. Hugh Missildine, *Your Inner Child of the Past* (New York: Simon & Schuster, 1968), concepts were adapted from chapter 13.

2. Nick Stinnet, Barbara Chesser, and John DeFrain, eds., *Building Family Strengths: Blueprint for Action* (Lincoln, Neb.: University of Nebraska Press, 1979), p. 112.

3. Missildine, *Your Inner Child,* pp. 143, 144.

4. John Powell, *The Secret of Staying in Love* (Niles, Ill: Argus Communications, 1974), p. 13.

5. Lawrence Crabb, *Effective Biblical Counseling* (Grand Rapids: Zondervan, 1977), pp. 83, 84.

Chapter 10

1.William J. Knaus, *Do It Now: How To Stop Procrastinating* (Englewood Cliffs, N. J.: Prentice Hall, 1979), p. 64.

2. Ibid, p. 70.

3. Peter M. Lewinsohn, Ricardo F. Munoz, Mary Ann Youngren, and Antoinette M. Zeiss, *Control Your Depression* (Englewood Cliffs, N. J.: Prentice Hall, 1979), pp. 175–177.

Chapter 11

1. Dr. George Weinberg, *Self Creation* (New York: Avon Books, 1978), adapted from p. 4.

2. Ibid., adapted from pp. 48–55.

3. Richard F. Berg and Christine McCartney, *Depression and the Integrated Life* (New York: Alba House, 1981), p. 34.

4. Ibid. p. 162.

5. Charles R. Swindoll, *Growing Strong in the Seasons of Life* (Portland, Ore.: Multnomah, 1983), p. 78.

6. Lloyd John Ogilvie, *God's Best for My Life* (Eugene, Ore.: Harvest House, 1981), March 3 daily reading.

CHRISTIAN HERALD ASSOCIATION AND ITS MINISTRIES

CHRISTIAN HERALD ASSOCIATION, founded in 1878, publishes The Christian Herald Magazine, one of the leading interdenominational religious monthlies in America. Through its wide circulation, it brings inspiring articles and the latest news of religious developments to many families. From the magazine's pages came the initiative for CHRISTIAN HERALD CHILDREN and THE BOWERY MISSION, two individually supported not-for-profit corporations.

CHRISTIAN HERALD CHILDREN, established in 1894, is the name for a unique and dynamic ministry to disadvantaged children, offering hope and opportunities which would not otherwise be available for reasons of poverty and neglect. The goal is to develop each child's potential and to demonstrate Christian compassion and understanding to children in need.

Mont Lawn is a permanent camp located in Bushkill, Pennsylvania. It is the focal point of a ministry which provides a healthful "vacation with a purpose" to children who without it would be confined to the streets of the city. Up to 1000 children between the age of 7 and 11 come to Mont Lawn each year.

Christian Herald Children maintains year-round contact with children by means of a *City Youth Ministry.* Central to its philosophy is the belief that only through sustained relationships and demonstrated concern can individual lives be truly enriched. Special emphasis is on individual guidance, spiritual and family counseling and tutoring. This follow-up ministry to inner-city children culminates for many in financial assistance toward higher education and career counseling.

THE BOWERY MISSION, located at 227 Bowery, New York City, has since 1879 been reaching out to the lost men on the Bowery, offering them what could be their last chance to rebuild their lives. Every man is fed, clothed and ministered to. Countless numbers have entered the 90-day residential rehabilitation program at the Bowery Mission. A concentrated ministry of counseling, medical care, nutrition therapy, Bible study and Gospel services awakens a man to spiritual renewal within himself.

These ministries are supported solely by the voluntary contributions of individuals and by legacies and bequests. Contributions are tax deductible. Checks should be made out either to CHRISTIAN HERALD CHILDREN or to THE BOWERY MISSION.

Administrative Office: 40 Overlook Drive, Chappaqua, New York 10514
Telephone: (914) 769-9000